Celebrating the Gift of Forgiveness

Sister Mary Fearon, RSM
Sandra J. Hirstein

Dubuque, Iowa

Name ______________________

Address ______________________

Phone ______________________

Nihil Obstat
Rev. Richard L. Schaefer

Imprimatur
+Most Rev. Daniel W. Kucera, OSB
Archbishop of Dubuque
15 January 1992

Book Team

Publisher—Ernest T. Nedder
Editor—Mary Jo Graham
Art Director—Cathy Frantz
Production Manager—Marilyn Rothenberger
Illustrator—Mary Beth Owens

Photo Credits

James L. Shaffer (cover and interior)

Bible Excerpts

ISBN 0-697-17629-0

20 19 18 17 16 15 14 13 12

Contents

A Note to Parents about the Sacrament of Reconciliation

All the sacraments are means of worshiping. They are ritual celebrations. Sometimes we adult Christians fail to recognize this fact, especially in regard to the Rite of Reconciliation. However, the concept of Reconciliation as something to celebrate and thank God for, is something that your children will easily appreciate and understand. They readily grasp the link between the admission of human weakness and praise for a forgiving Father who is always ready to welcome them back.

Sin and the Young Child

Although their ability to understand the nature of sin is extremely limited at this point in their lives, children are familiar with the experience of disharmony. They feel alienation, and it is sin that is at the root of all alienation. At a very early age, children respond to this alienation within the context of their own families. They know when something is amiss. They sense disharmony. Even though they may not use the term *sin*, children will frequently feel the separation and alienation that has its roots in sin.

This inability to fully grasp the nature of sinful actions, to identify sin, does not prevent young children from understanding the importance of reconciliation.

As a child matures, the free flowing, unspecified sense of alienation will give way to a more defined sense of right and wrong. Learning how to discern sinful acts and attitudes in one's own life is an important part of the formation of conscience. A priest-confessor takes a real and direct part in this formation as it occurs in an individual. Early participation in the Sacrament of Reconciliation will enable a confessor to help direct your child's conscience formation even before serious sin becomes a question.

Developing an Understanding of Reconciliation

It is important for both parents and catechists, and parents as catechists, to realize that the understandings that are basic to the celebration of the Sacrament of Reconciliation are also those that are most basic to the development of the Christian person. Primary in these understandings is a recognition of God as Father. Secondly, children must know that the Father is good. It is this knowledge that enables the children to leap from a vague realization that something is amiss in their relationship with God to an acknowledgment that the lack must be theirs and not God's. The child then experiences weakness or sin as his or her own.

Acknowledging one's sinfulness and reconciling that weakness with the intrinsic goodness of oneself is not easy. Within a human family, a child discovers failings at an early age. Children discover the actions that are displeasing to those they love, the things that cause dissension and result in a lack of harmony. Yet children can accept their part in these actions simply because a good parent makes it perfectly clear that the child is loved even if some actions the child performs are not good.

Because of this attitude, children intuit their basic goodness. Within the Church, this same sense of worthiness must be established. The child's admission of weakness is given with the hope of reassurance and acceptance (or forgiveness), since this is how the child has experienced love within the family. Without the experience of forgiveness, the child has little reassurance of worth. Children must know that they are good, that some of their actions deny this goodness, and that God will always forgive and continuously love them. This is not three separate realizations, but one.

Implications for Your Family

1. Parents have a need and a responsibility to grow in an understanding of the Sacrament of Reconciliation within the adult community. It is important for their faith development, and it is important for the faith of the children within their family.
2. The role of forgiveness in human life must be highlighted. "Forgiveness moments" within the family should be marked and celebrated.
3. The family should regard the Rite of Reconciliation as a positive encounter deserving of celebration.

Conclusion

Many adults today regret the negative emotions that the Sacrament of Reconciliation produces within them. It is not too late to overcome these emotions. By taking a positive approach to the Sacrament of Reconciliation with their children, parents can also come to know this sacrament as the loving embrace of an ever welcoming Father who continuously loves them.

This material has previously appeared in
Focus on Belonging by Mary Jo Tully and Sandra Hirstein.

For Parents: 1 God's Love Welcomes Us
Lesson Focus: Loving
Goal: To help your child become more aware of how much God loves His children and how Jesus and the Church show God's love.
Summary: Jesus gave us many signs of His love. Jesus' Church gives us signs of love, too. One sign is the Sacrament of Reconciliation. *Reconciliation* means "to bring together again." Reconciliation brings forgiveness and peace. It brings us closer to Jesus. In the Sacrament of Reconciliation, the priest speaks in the name of Jesus and Jesus' Church.
Sacramental Focus: The Sacrament of Reconciliation is a sign of God's forgiving love.
Scripture Focus: "I will never forget you; I have written your name on the palms of my hands." (Isaiah 49:16)
Reflection: The most important need that the young child has is to be loved and to feel loved. Only when the child feels secure in the love of those who are important in his or her life, can that child reach out and respond to life's new challenges. That is why it is important that the child be given tangible signs of love by those who care for him or her. These tangible signs need not be material objects. They may be hugs or affectionate squeezes or your willingness to play catch "one more time."

You can help your child, through giving these signs of love, to better understand the free gift of God's love. It is God who has called each of us into being. He is the Father who has loved us beyond reason, who has loved us first, who has loved us before we were able to do anything deserving of love. Nor will the Father ever stop loving us. He loves for always and ever. He loves us as we are and as we can become through His love. His love is everlasting.

The Father has shown us many tangible signs of His love. He has given us the extraordinary world in which we live and the people who love us. He has given us His great gift, Jesus. One of the signs of God's love is the Sacrament of Reconciliation. Reconciliation comes about because God is always willing to receive us in love.

Before we receive the Sacrament of Reconciliation, the priest welcomes us in Jesus' name. His welcome is a sign of God's love. It is a sign that God will never forget us. Just as God is willing to forgive us, so must we be willing to forgive our brothers and sisters.

1 God's Love Welcomes Us

St. Martin

St. Martin was only fifteen years old when he decided that he wanted to follow Jesus. But, as a young man, he was forced into the army.

One very cold winter night, he was standing guard at the city gate. He saw a poor man, dressed in thin, shabby clothes, begging help from passers-by. They pushed him aside.

Martin had no money. He had only his weapons and a thick army cloak. He thought for a moment. Then he took his sword and cut the cloak in two. He gave one half to the poor man.

That night in a dream, Martin saw Jesus. He was wearing Martin's cloak. Martin heard Jesus say, "Martin has covered me with his cloak."

How did St. Martin show love?

St. Margaret

St. Margaret was the mother of eight children. She was also queen of Scotland. The people loved their queen because she was so kind.

Once Margaret met a poor woman with a baby. "How beautiful your baby is!" said Margaret. "Yes," said the mother, "but how can I feed her? I have no money."

Margaret took the child in her arms. She gently rocked the baby. After some time, she gave the child back to her mother.

After the queen left, the mother found a surprise. Hidden in the folds of the baby's blanket were ten large gold coins—enough to feed the baby for a year!

How did St. Margaret show love?

Love Shows Itself

There are many ways that people show love.

Name two ways that people who love you show their love.

____

____

Name two ways that you can show someone that you care.

____

____

God the Father loves you.

His Son Jesus loves you, too.

The Bible tells many stories about Jesus' love for people.

Jesus Welcomes the Children

One day Jesus was very tired. He sat down to rest. Some parents brought their children to Jesus. They wanted Jesus to lay His hands in blessing upon the children.

The apostles did not like that.

They wanted Jesus to rest, so they tried to keep the children away.

But Jesus loves children.

He told the apostles,

"Let the little children come to Me.

Don't stop them."

Then Jesus reached out and welcomed the children to Himself. (See Mark 10:13–16.)

Reconciliation—Sign of Love

Jesus gave us many signs of His love.

Jesus' Church gives us signs of love, too.

One sign is the Sacrament of Reconciliation.

The word *reconciliation* means "to bring together again."

The Sacrament of Reconciliation is a sign of God's forgiving love.

It brings forgiveness and peace.

Bible Search—
Read these verses in your Bible—
Mark 10:13–16.
What did Jesus say belongs to those who are like children, who come to Jesus in love?

____

____

Reconciliation—To bring together again.

It brings us closer to Jesus and to one another.

At the celebration of reconciliation, the priest takes Jesus' place.

He speaks in the name of Jesus and of Jesus' Church.

He welcomes us.

He asks us to trust in God's love.

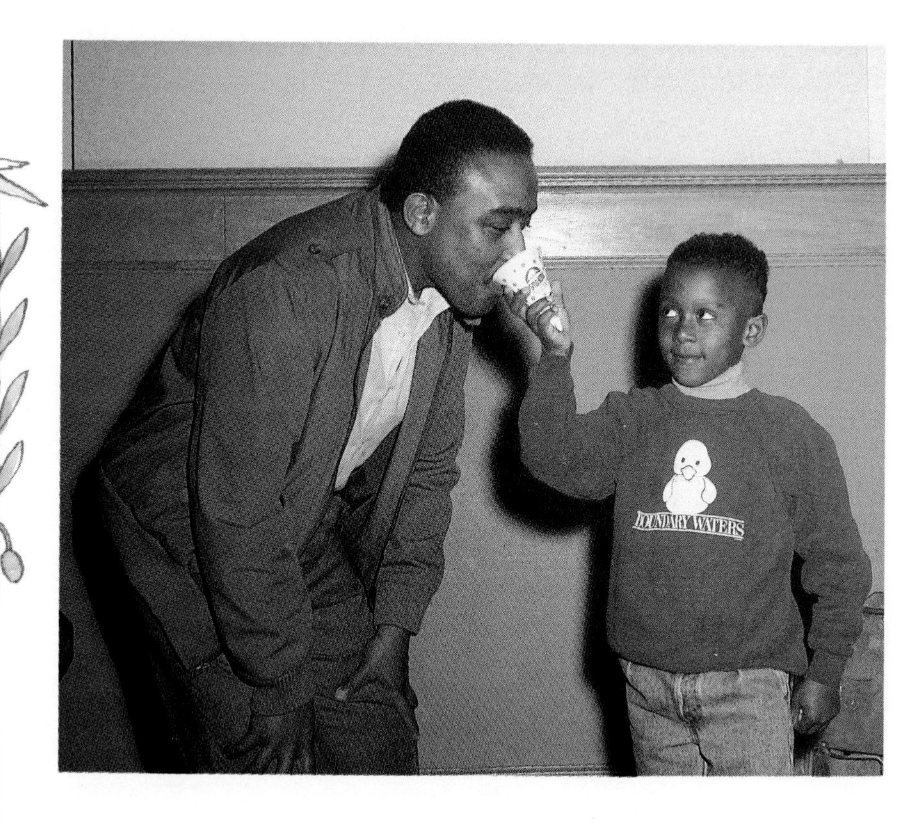

God Loves Us

When we celebrate the Sacrament of Reconciliation, we remember that God loves us and will never turn away from us when we ask for forgiveness.

In the Bible, God tells us:

"I can never forget you!
I have written your name on
the palms of My hands."

(Isaiah 49:16)

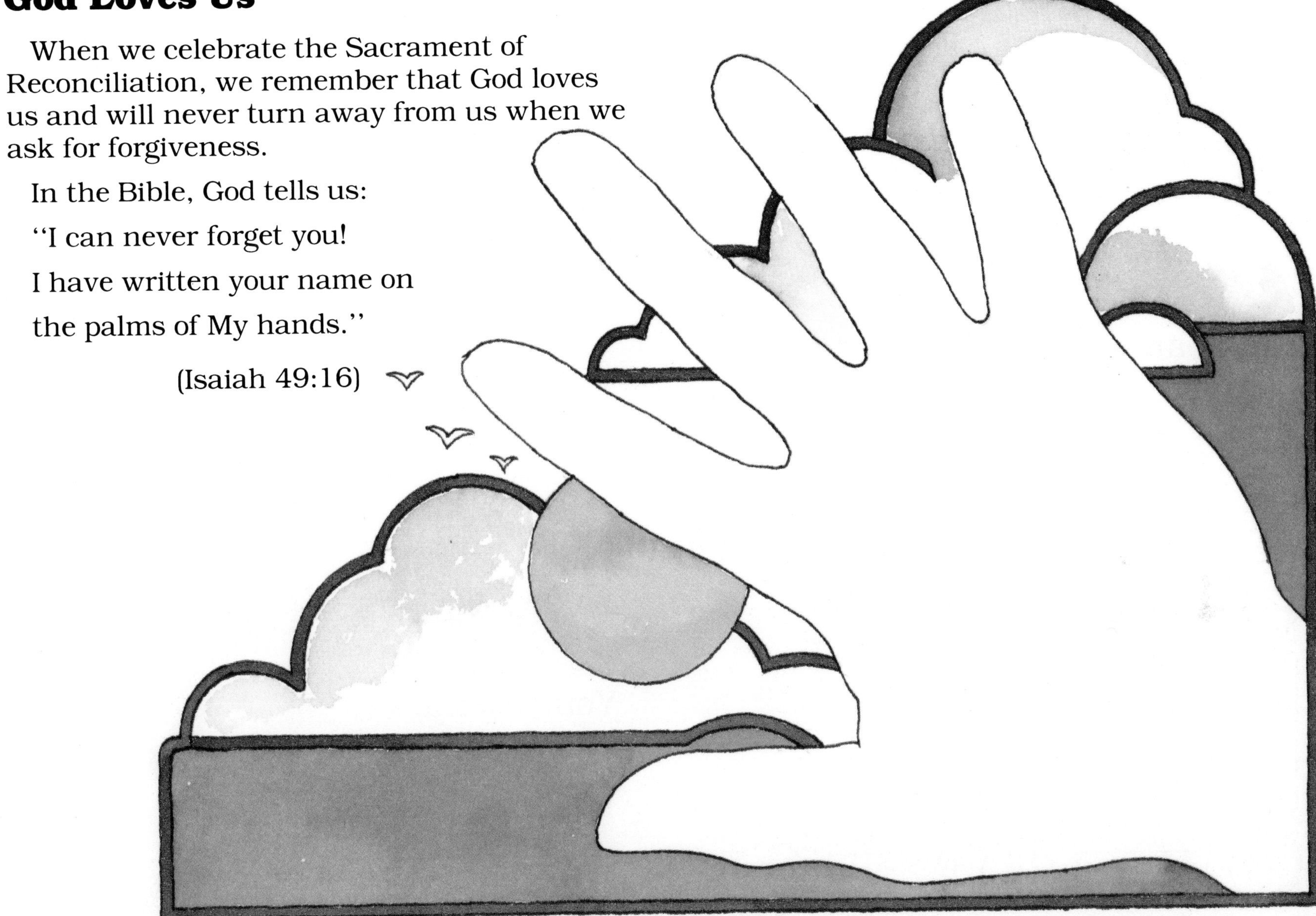

Trace your hand inside the big hand on this page. Write your name in the middle of the hands.

Dear ____________________

I would like to celebrate God's gift of love and forgiveness, the Sacrament of Reconciliation.

I am ____ years old and in the ____ grade at ____________________________________ .

One special gift that God gave to me is _______________________ .

I will share with others the gifts God gives me.

One thing I will do to show my love for God and God's people is ____

Your friend,

____

Review Sheet 1 God's Love Welcomes Us

Words to Know

Reconciliation means ____ .

Questions to Answer

1. What do we call the sacrament of God's forgiving love?

____

2. What does the Sacrament of Reconciliation bring?

____

3. In whose name does the priest speak?

____

Scripture to Remember

God says:

"I can never forget __________ !

I have written your __________ on the __________ of my hands." (Isaiah 49:16)

Jesus says:

"Let the little children __________ to Me. Don't stop them." (Mark 10:14)

Review

Take time to discuss these questions with your child.

- Who are some people who love you?
- How do you know? (What signs of love do they give you?)
- Who made you because He loved you?
- Whom did God the Father send to show His love for people?
- How did Jesus show love for people?
- Can you tell me the story of how Jesus welcomed the children?
- What does the word *reconciliation* mean?
- What is the name that the Church gives to the sacrament of forgiveness?
- Who welcomes you in the name of Jesus and the Church?
- What does God show you through the Sacrament of Reconciliation?

Centering Prayer

Find a quiet time to lead your child in a guided meditation on Scripture.

1. Help your child to relax by taking time for slow, deep breathing.
2. Read the meditation slowly, giving the child time to recreate the Gospel scene.
3. Give sufficient time for personal prayer.

God's Love Welcomes Us (See Mark 10:13–16)

Close your eyes. Place your hands on your knees. Sit very quiet and breath slowly and deeply. Come along to meet Jesus. Jesus is sitting down to rest under a tree in a beautiful park. Feel the cool air and warm sunshine. Hear the birds singing. Listen to the many voices of people talking and laughing. Many parents are bringing children over to Jesus. You are with your family and are walking over to Jesus. All of a sudden, you hear friends of Jesus say, "Take the children away. Jesus is tired. He needs rest."

Jesus says to His friends, "Let the little children come to Me. Don't stop them." Many children run over to Jesus. Jesus hugs the children. Then you hear Jesus call you by name. You run over to Jesus and stand in front of Him. Jesus takes your hands in His and looks deep into your eyes. Jesus says, "N. ________ I love you. I welcome you and will be with you always." You feel close to Jesus. You feel you belong. You thank Jesus and tell Him how you love Him and want to receive Him.

Now I will give you time to pray to Jesus. (Be silent for a few minutes).

You hug Jesus. You wave good-bye and say, "Jesus, bless me always." Now open your eyes.

Action

As time allows, choose one or more of the activities given to reinforce the focus of the lesson.

Pray the Lord's Prayer together as a family. After saying Grace before the meal, add this special prayer: "Let us all bless, N. ________ , who is preparing to celebrate God's gift of reconciliation."

Plan to be present at the parent meeting to deepen your own understanding of the Sacrament of Reconciliation. Send your child's catechist a snapshot of your child. This will enable the catechist to display the pictures of those children who will be preparing for the Sacrament of Reconciliation, so that the whole parish will be aware of them and keep them in their prayers.

Resources

Children

The Runaway Bunny by Margaret Wise Brown (New York: Harper and Row, 1942).

Whobody There? by Charles and Ann Morse (Nashville, TN: Upper Room, 1977).

Adults

Christian Parenting, the Young Child (Mahwah, NJ: Paulist Press, 1980).

Healing Life's Hurts by Dennis and Matthew Linn (Mahwah, NJ: Paulist Press, 1977).

To Walk Together Again by Richard M. Gula, SS (New York: Paulist Press, 1983).

For Parents: 2 God's Forgiveness Makes Us One
Lesson Focus: Belonging
Goal: To help children understand that through the Sacrament of Baptism they belong to God's Christian family, the Church, and that through the Sacrament of Reconciliation they can always be a part of that family, even when they fail.
Summary: Baptism is an effective sign that we belong to God's Christian family, the Church. We were brought into that family through the waters of baptism, in the name of the Father, Son, and Holy Spirit. The Sacrament of Reconciliation is an effective sign that we will always be welcome in that family, even when we fail to do what God asks.
Sacramental Focus: We begin the celebration of the Sacrament of Reconciliation by making the Sign of the Cross, a sign that means that we belong to our loving Father's Christian family.
Scripture Focus: "I am the Lord who created you; from the time you were born, I have helped you. . . . Do not be afraid—I will save you. I have called you by name—you are Mine." (Isaiah 44:2; 43:1)
Reflection: The first experience of belonging—of identification with a group—occurs within the context of the family. If this experience is positive, young children begin to develop a basic sense of security that can sustain them throughout life. Children who experience the goodness of belonging to their family will transfer this goodness to themselves. They will see themselves as worthwhile because they belong to a family that is good. They will recognize that they are valuable because their family values them. By nurturing their self-esteem, the family gives its members the confidence that ultimately enables them to reach out to others.

You can help your child to develop this confidence by giving signs that show that you value his or her unique contributions to the family. If you recognize a particular talent or ability or skill in your child, tell him or her that you have noticed it. Listen to your child with the same respect that you would show to an adult member of your family. Offer your child responsibilities within the family. Doing so says to your child that you believe in and trust him or her. When your young child tries and fails, reassure him or her with a warm hug, or with verbal encouragement.

It is important that children feel that they belong to the family even when they fail to measure up to the family's demands. This confidence forms the basis upon which they will be able to celebrate the Sacrament of Reconciliation. Children must first believe in their own forgivability before they will take advantage of the Christian community's offer of forgiveness in the Sacrament of Reconciliation.

Through the Sacrament of Baptism, the Christian knows that he or she belongs to God's family, the Church. Through the Sacrament of Reconciliation, the Christian knows that he or she can always be a part of that family.

2 God's Forgiveness Makes Us One

You have a special family name. Your name shows that you belong to your family.

What is your family name? Print it in the center of the flower.

Who belongs to your family?

Print their names on the flower.

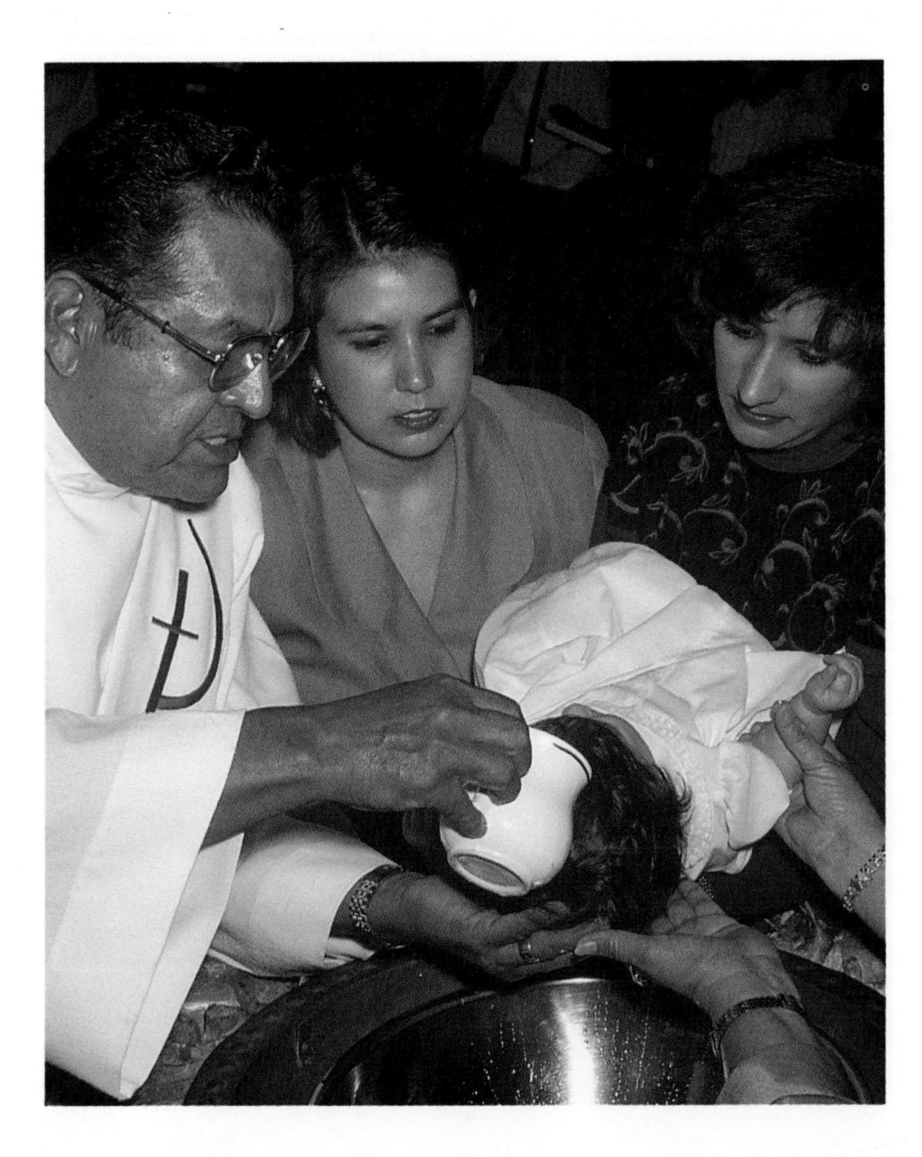

Christians Together

Your baptism shows that you belong to another family, too.

You are part of God's Christian family, the Church.

At your baptism, you were given a Christian name. The priest said, "I baptize you in the name of the Father, and of the Son, and of the Holy Spirit."

Your baptism is a sign that you belong to the Christian family. There will always be a place for you in this family.

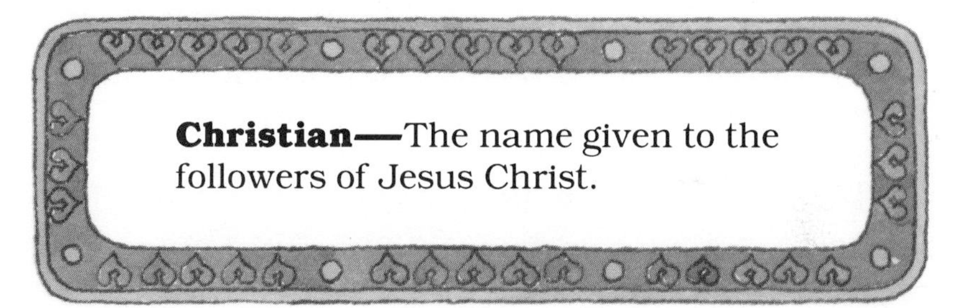

Christian—The name given to the followers of Jesus Christ.

Did You Know?
A custom among Catholics is to give a newborn child a saint's name at baptism. Parents do so in hope that the saint will be the child's special patron or protector. While Catholic parents do not have to follow this custom, many do. Do you have a patron saint?

The Unhappy Son

One day, Jesus told a story about a loving father who had two sons. One son was satisfied to be at home with his family, but the other son was tired of it.

The unhappy son asked his father to give him his share of the family money. He wanted to get away from his family, so he could do whatever he wanted to do. The father was very sad to see his son leave home.

The unhappy son went far away. He spent his money on "having a good time." While he had money, he had many friends. But when his money ran out, so did his friends.

The young man was hungry and alone. He looked for a job so he could eat, but there were no good jobs to be had.

At last he found a job on a pig farm. He didn't like the job, and he still was hungry. Sometimes he was so hungry that he even ate what the pigs left.

Then he began to think about what he had done.

He remembered how kind his father was. He felt sorry that he had left home and wasted the money his father had given him. He felt very sorry because he had hurt his father who loved him. He decided to go back home and ask his father's forgiveness. He said to himself, "I will ask my father to take me back as a hired man."

All the while his son was gone, the father had watched for the son's return. One day, while he was looking far down the road, the father saw his son. The father ran to meet him. How the father and son hugged one another!

That night the father ordered a big celebration. He invited everyone to the party to share the joy. He said, "My son is home again!" (See Luke 15:11–24)

God Forgives

Sometimes we are like the unhappy son. We act selfishly. We hurt the people who love us. We choose to do wrong. When that happens, we know that we can receive forgiveness. One way is through the Sacrament of Reconciliation.

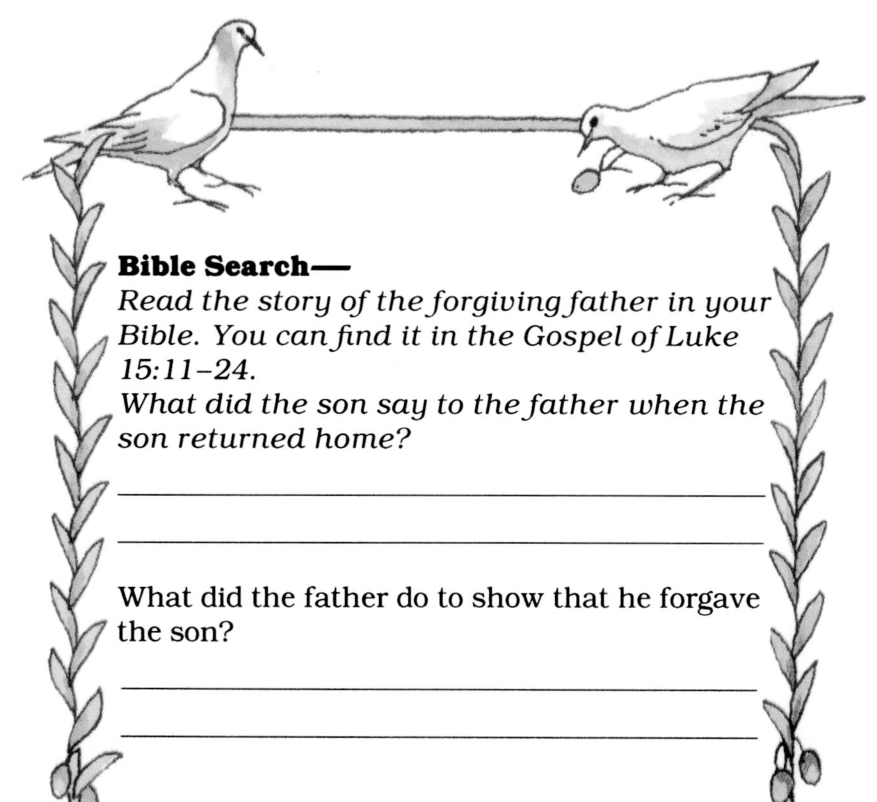

Bible Search—
Read the story of the forgiving father in your Bible. You can find it in the Gospel of Luke 15:11–24.
What did the son say to the father when the son returned home?

____

____

What did the father do to show that he forgave the son?

____

____

The Sacrament of Reconciliation is a way in which those who belong to Jesus can find peace and forgiveness.

The Sign of the Cross

When we celebrate reconciliation, we begin by praying the Sign of the Cross. It reminds us that we are the children of a loving God. We belong to God's Christian family.

What sign reminds us that we have been baptized in God's name and belong to God's Christian family?

Can you think of some times when you pray the Sign of the Cross?

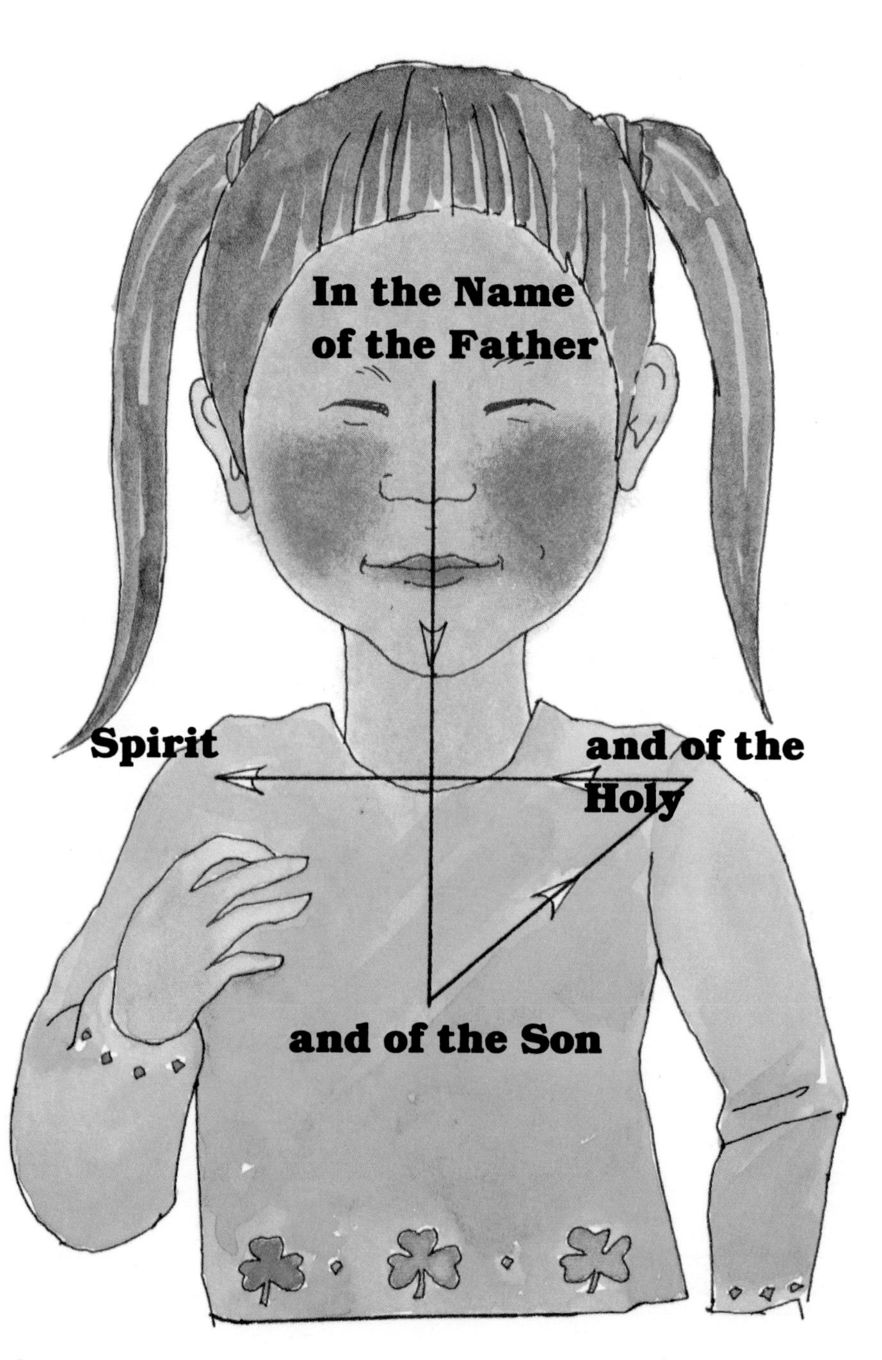

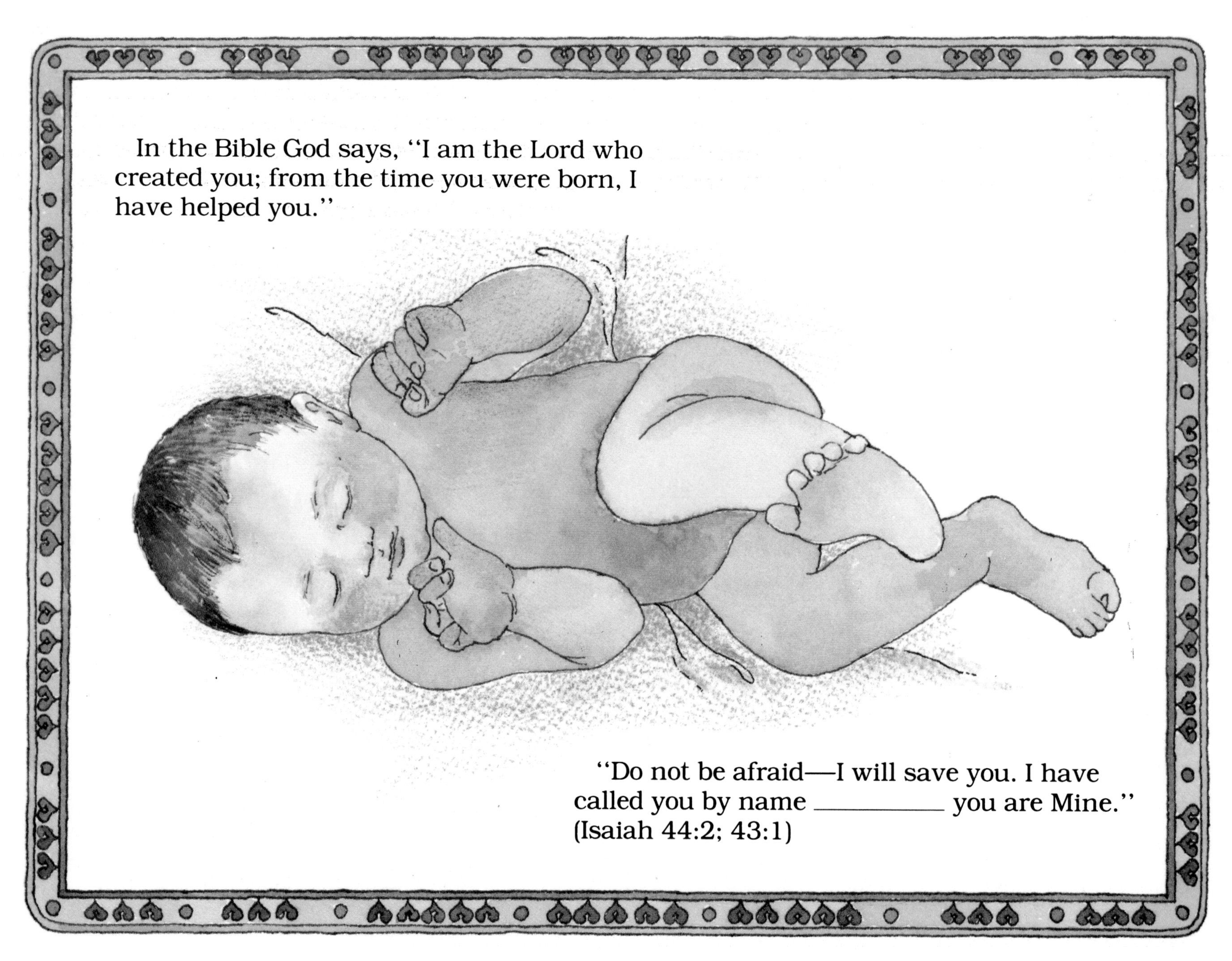

In the Bible God says, "I am the Lord who created you; from the time you were born, I have helped you."

"Do not be afraid—I will save you. I have called you by name __________ you are Mine." (Isaiah 44:2; 43:1)

God Promises His Love Forever

Dear God,

I am Your child.
Thank You for my f ______________ .

Thank you for making me a part of
Your Christian family, the C _________ ,
through b ______________ .

Thank you for

____

____ .

family baptism Church

Color the rainbow.

Review Sheet 2: God's Forgiveness Makes Us One

Words to Know

Christian means ______________________________

Questions to Answer

1. Through what sacrament did you become a part of God's Christian family, the Church?

____

2. Of what does the Sign of the Cross remind us?

____

Scripture to Remember

God says:

"I have called you by __________—you are __________." (Isaiah 43:1)

The Story of the Forgiving Father (Luke 15:11–24)

Read the following sentences. Put them in the order in which they happened in Luke's story.

_____ The father gives his son his inheritance.

_____ The son decides to leave his home and family.

_____ The son receives his father's love and forgiveness.

_____ The son tells his father that he has done wrong.

_____ The son wastes his money foolishly and ends up penniless.

_____ The son thinks about his father's love.

_____ The son decides to go home and ask for forgiveness.

Review

Take time to discuss these questions with your child.

- What do you like about belonging to our family?
- What are some of the good things we do as a family?
- When did you become a member of our family?
- When did you become a member of God's Christian family, the Church?
- What would you like to know about your baptism?
- What sign do Christians make that reminds them that they believe in Jesus?
- Can you pray the Sign of the Cross with me?
- Can you tell me the story about the son who left his home and about the forgiving father?
- Of what does the Sign of the Cross remind us?
- Can you name some times when we pray the Sign of the Cross?

Centering Prayer

Find a quiet time to lead your child in a guided meditation on Scripture.

1. Help your child to relax by taking time for slow, deep breathing.
2. Read the meditation slowly, giving the child time to recreate the Gospel scene.
3. Give sufficient time for personal prayer.

The Forgiving Father (See Luke 15:11–24)

Close your eyes. Take a deep breath. Relax. You are walking along a dirt road that leads to a huge farm house. In front of the house, you see a group of people sitting under a shady elm tree. You see a person get up and leave the group. He is coming down the road toward you. As the person comes near you, you hear him calling your name. You look up and see it is Jesus.

Jesus says, "N ________ , would you like to join our group to listen to the story about a loving Father?" You feel excited and reply, "Yes, yes, I would, Jesus!" Jesus takes your hand and brings you over to the group and introduces you. In the group, you see some children your own age. They invite you to sit down beside them. You sit down right in front of Jesus.

Jesus begins:

"There was once a loving father who had two sons. One son was contented to be at home. But the other was discontented and restless. He wanted to leave. The unhappy son asked his father to give him his share of the family money. The kind father got the share and gave it to his son. The father was very sad to see his son leave home.

The unhappy son went far, far away. He spent his money on having a 'good time.' But soon the money ran out. He was broke! While he had money, he had lots of friends; but when his money was gone so were his friends.

"The young man felt alone and hungry. He had no friends, no home, no money, and was without a job. He did find a job feeding the pigs, but he was not very happy and didn't make very much money. He still was hungry and often ate 'leftovers' from the pigs.

"The whole situation was getting to him! One day he began to think about what he had done. He remembered his kind Father. He said, 'I will ask my father to take me back as a hired man.'

"The son came home. How happy the father and the son were to be reunited. The loving father and son hugged each other. The loving father said, 'Let's have a party. My son who was lost is now found. My son is home again! Celebrate with me and my family!' "

Jesus now turns to you. He takes your hands. He looks into your eyes and says, "The father in My story is like My Father in heaven who loves you so much that He is always waiting to forgive you. He always welcomes you. He loves you even when you fail. He is waiting to embrace you. How does that make you feel?"

I will give you a quiet time so that you can talk to Jesus about this. (Pause for silent prayer.)

It's time to leave Jesus. Give Jesus a hug. Get up and begin to walk back down the road. Turn and wave good-bye to Jesus and the group of people.

Open your eyes and come back into the room.

Action

As time allows, choose one or more of the activities given to reinforce the focus of the lesson.

Make a cross on your child's forehead before sending him or her to school or at bedtime. A blessing is a way of praising God for His goodness. You can make this a meaningful ritual in your own home.

The cross is a universal symbol of Christianity. Point out to your child the crosses marking neighboring churches in your area. Become aware of the names of the ministers of the Churches in your area. Offer a prayer for the people of these Churches. (Note that not all churches have such a cross.)

Resources

Children

The Selfish Giant by Oscar Wilde (New York: Harvey House, 1967).

What Kind of Family Is This? by Barbara Seuling (Racine, WI: Western Publishing Company, 1985).

Adult

The Living Reminder by Henri J. M. Nouwen (New York: Seabury Press, 1977).

Hope for Healing by George Leach (Mahwah, NJ: Paulist Press, 1966).

For Parents: 3 God's Word Guides Us
Lesson Focus: Listening
Goal: To help your child become better attuned to listening to God's Word in his or her life.
Summary: God speaks to us through creation, through the Bible, through the Church, through the everyday events of our lives, through other persons, and especially through the person of Jesus. We must learn to take time to listen to God's Word of love in our lives. God's Word can show us how to live a happy life.
Sacramental Focus: In the Sacrament of Reconciliation, we take time to listen to God's Word in the Bible. Our priest proclaims God's Word while we listen carefully and let it touch our hearts.
Scripture Focus: "Happy are all those who hear the word of God and put it into practice." (Luke 11:28)
Reflection: Contemporary research into listening suggests that most of us are not very good listeners. Generally, it is not that there is anything wrong with our ability to hear. We simply fail to recognize that listening demands that we hear with more than our ears. To hear well, we must listen with our ears and our eyes, with our hearts and our minds—with our whole person. Indeed, we can open our ears to every word that another person says, but if we close our minds and hearts to the other's whole person, we may never hear the message.

Our listening patterns are established when we are very young and are heavily influenced by the listening habits of the people close to us—our families. You are now passing your listening habits onto your children. Take some time to reflect on the way you listen to your children. Do you give real attention to what your child says, or are you listening with your ears, while your mind is planning what you will pick up at the hardware store? Do you listen respectfully to your child, or do you have a tendency to stereotype and dismiss his or her contributions as childish prattle? Are you alert to what your child's body language, eye contact, and vocal inflection are also conveying? Do you show your child by an appropriate response that you have heard what he or she has said?

By modeling good listening habits for your children, you are equipping them to better hear the Word of God in their own lives. Hearing the Word of God demands that we listen with our whole person to the many and varied ways in which God speaks to us as unique individuals, through creation, through Scripture, through Jesus, through the Church, and through the events of our own lives.

The Sacrament of Reconciliation gives us such a chance to listen to God's Word. How well we have heard it will be evident in our actions.

3 God's Word Guides Us

St. Francis and the Wolf

Once a fierce wolf lived near the town of Gubio. He had killed many sheep, and even some cattle. His sharp teeth and terrible growls frightened all the people of the village. Some brave villagers set out a few times to kill the wolf, but they could never find him.

One day, St. Francis came to Gubio. Francis had no money, but he owned a happy heart, filled with love for all God's creatures. Francis had a good word for everyone, and the villagers were always glad to see him.

The people told Francis about the wolf and how he could not be found. Francis listened closely. Then he said, "Let's go see that wolf." The people followed Francis, wondering what he would do.

Francis called the wolf. He called again, and then again. Soon the people saw the wolf standing on a far-off hill, his sharp teeth shining. Francis called again. The people cried out in fear as the wolf charged.

He came to a stop at Francis' feet. Francis bent down, close to the wolf's face. He said, "Brother Wolf, I am glad you are here. But the people of Gubio are not. They are very afraid of you. You must stop scaring them. God loves them even as he loves you. If you are kind to them, they will be kind to you. If you trust them, they will trust you."

Then Francis stretched out his hand to the wolf, and the wolf put his paw in the saint's hand.

From that day on, the wolf and the townspeople were friends. The people cared for the wolf, and he protected them. When at last, the wolf died, the villagers cried as if for a brother.

What did St. Francis say to the wolf?

What did the wolf do to show that he would do as Francis asked?

God's Words of Love

God wants people to know that He cares about them.

God speaks His words of love in many ways—through His creation, through His holy book, the Bible, through His Church, through the people in our lives, and especially through His Son Jesus. God sent His Son Jesus to speak His love.

Bible—A special book, often called the "Word of God," through which God tells people about Himself.

How does God speak to us?

Unscramble these words:

LEBBI

TREACNIO

PLOPEE

SUSJE

HUCCRH

It is important to listen to Jesus' words. Jesus wants His friends to listen.

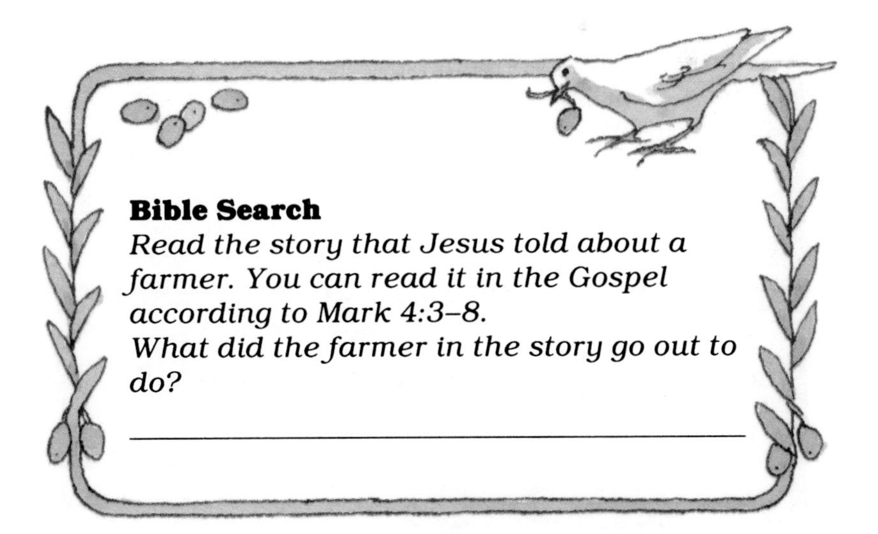

Bible Search
Read the story that Jesus told about a farmer. You can read it in the Gospel according to Mark 4:3–8.
What did the farmer in the story go out to do?

____

God's Word—Seed within Us

After you have heard the story of the farmer (see Mark 4:3–8), answer each question by drawing a line from the question to its answer.

Some seed fell on hard ground. What happened to it?	It grew and grew and grew.
Some seed fell on rocky ground. What happened to it?	Birds ate it.
Some seed fell among weeds. What happened to it?	It died for lack of water.
Some seed fell on good soil. What happened to it?	It was crowded out and choked off.

Jesus tells us that the seed stands for the Word of God. The good soil stands for the hearts of those who hear God's W _ _ _ and keep it.

Listening to God's Word

When we celebrate the Sacrament of Penance and Reconciliation, we should take some time to listen to God's Word. We can do it before we talk with the priest. Or, after welcoming us, our priest may read to us from God's Word, the Bible. Whenever God's Word is read, we must listen to it carefully. We must let it touch our hearts.

In the Gospel according to Saint Luke, Jesus tells us, "Happy are all who hear the Word of God and put it into practice." (Luke 11:28)

Did You Know?
The most popular book of all time is the Bible. More copies of the Bible have been sold than of any other book.

The Bible—Word of God

Design a cover for a Bible. Use a drawing, a symbol, or words—or a combination of all.

Review Sheet 3: God's Word Guides Us

Words to Know

The Bible is ____.

Questions to Answer

1. What are some ways in which God speaks to us?

____

2. What is another name for the Bible?

____

Scripture to Remember

Can you decode this message? Find the letter that corresponds to the number. Write the letter in the space above the number. When you finish you will have a saying of Jesus that is found in Luke 11:28.

“H _ _ _ y   a _ _   _ l _   w _ _   _ _ _ r
1 2 3 3 15   2 4 5   2 17 17   7 1 8   1 5 2 4

_ _ _   _ _ _ _   _ f   G _ _   _ n d   p u _
6 1 5   7 8 4 9   8 10   11 8 9   2 12 9   3 13 6

_ t   i _ _ o   _ _ _ c _ _ c e.” (Luke 11:28)
14 6   14 12 6 8   3 4 2 16 6 14 16 5

Review

Take time to discuss these questions with your child.

- What are some things that you like to hear?
- What are some ways God speaks to us?
- Can you tell me the story of the sower who planted some seed?
- What did Jesus say the seed stood for?
- What did Jesus say the good soil stood for?
- Can you tell me about a Bible story that you have heard that you like?
- During the Sacrament of Reconciliation, if the priest reads from the Word of God, the Bible, what should you do?

Centering Prayer

Find a quiet time to lead your child in a guided meditation on Scripture.

1. Help your child to relax by taking time for slow, deep breathing.
2. Read the meditation slowly, giving the child time to recreate the Gospel scene.
3. Give sufficient time for personal prayer.

God's Word Guides Us (Parable of Sower and Seed) (Mark 4:3–8)

Close your eyes. Take a deep breath and relax. You are by a lake. You are with Jesus. A huge crowd gathers around Jesus. Jesus sees you standing near the lake with the huge crowd. Jesus takes your hand and helps you into a boat. You sit right next to Jesus. Jesus says, "Let's row out a little from the crowd. In this way, the crowd can better hear what I have to teach."

Jesus and you are sitting in the boat and are facing the crowd. Jesus looks down at you; then He looks out at the crowd. He says loud and clear: "Listen carefully to this! (You close your eyes and try to paint a picture in your mind as Jesus tells the story about a farmer planting seeds.)

"A farmer went out sowing seeds. Some of the seeds landed on the foot path, where the birds came along and ate them. Some of the seeds landed on rocky ground where there was very little soil; this seed sprouted immediately because the soil had no depth. Then when the sun rose and scorched it, the seed began to wither for lack of roots. Some landed on thorns that grew up and choked it off, and there was no yield of grain. Some seed finally landed on good soil and yielded grain that sprang up to produce at the rate of thirty and sixty and a hundredfold." Jesus raised His arms and finished His parable by saying, "Let him who has ears to hear me, hear!"

Now you see the crowd moving away. Some of the people are trying to understand what Jesus said. They are talking among themselves. Many did not understand Jesus. Finally, the disciples, Jesus and you are left alone. Jesus walks right in front of you. He stands there, resting His hands on your shoulders. He looks deep into your eyes and heart. Jesus says, "The seed stands for the Word of God. The good soil stands for the hearts of those who hear God's Word and keep it. N_ , do you believe in Me? Will you listen to My words and try to put them into practice?" I will give you time now to speak with Jesus. (Pause for silent prayer.)

Now open your eyes and come back into the room.

Action

As time allows, choose one or more of the activities given to reinforce the focus of the lesson.

Before bed, or during some other quiet time, read a Bible story with your child. Talk about it together.

When do you find time to really listen to your child? Take a little time to discover something about your child that you did not know. Single out a whole day, or a briefer period, in which you can do something together.

A parish community must learn to listen to the needs of the neighborhood. Is there any small way your family can reach out to another family or person who has just suffered a loss? (Even a phone call is a listening sign of love.)

Resources

Children

The Child's Bible (Mahwah, NJ: Paulist Press, 1980).

If You Listen by Charlotte Zolotow (New York: Harper and Row, 1980).

Adults

Gifts from the Sea by Ann Morrow Lindberg (New York: Pantheon, 1955).

Parent Effectiveness Training in Action by Dr. Thomas Gordon (New York: Wyden, 1978).

Listen to Love by Louis M. Savary (New York: Regina Press, 1970).

For Parents: 4 We Follow God's Word
Lesson Focus: Following
Goal: To help your child become aware that when Christians love God and one another, they are following Jesus.
Summary: If we want to follow Jesus, we must love God and one another. Sometimes we fail—we sin. We come to know how we fail by listening to God's Word and examining our conscience. During the Sacrament of Reconciliation, we have a chance to listen to God's Word, the Bible.
Sacramental Focus: In the Sacrament of Reconciliation, after we listen to God's Word in the Bible, we ask ourselves how we have followed God's Word in our lives. We examine our conscience.
Scripture Focus: "If anyone wants to come with me, he must forget himself . . . and follow me." (Luke 9:23)
Reflection: Children are great imitators—as any parent will both happily and ruefully admit. Imitation is a basic part of the learning process. Moreover, the child is learning more than can be outwardly observed. As children imitate what they hear and see, they are also assimilating the attitudes and values of their models.

In order to help your child assimilate those behaviors, attitudes, and values consistent with the Christian lifestyle, think about the factors involved in the modeling process. (1) Attention—A child's attention to a model's behavior is heavily influenced by the person of the model. Warm, vibrant, powerful people command more attention than their opposites. (2) Retention—Children will better retain something that they have observed if they verbally rehearse the behavior. (3) Incentive—A child must perceive the behavior as rewarding in some way. (4) Level of development—The reproduction of a behavior must be within the child's physical, psychological, and spiritual capabilities.

In light of these factors, what can parents do? (1) Provide your child with role models who are warm, loving, and secure human beings. (2) Ask your child to verbally describe a behavior you want him or her to repeat. (3) Reward behavior you want repeated. The reward might be a word of encouragement or approval or a hug or a smile. (4) Do not demand that your child respond in a manner that is beyond his or her capabilities. Establish realistic expectations for your child.

Learning to follow Jesus is no easy task. Scripture helps us to better understand the Person of Jesus and His message, but living according to the message is the difficult part. We need to recognize that in this process of becoming Christian, we sometimes fail. When we do, the Christian community offers us support and encouragement through the Sacrament of Reconciliation. In the Sacrament of Reconciliation, after attending to God's Word, we have the opportunity to ask ourselves how we have followed God's Word in our lives. Reconciliation can help us to better follow Jesus by helping us to better understand how to love God and one another.

4 We Follow God's Word

Justin Chooses

Friday was popcorn day at school. For twenty-five cents, students could buy a bag at recess. Justin loved popcorn. But that Friday morning he forgot his quarter.

Justin saw a quarter laying on the top right corner of Ramon's desk. When Ramon was not looking, Justin took the quarter. At recess, Ramon found that his quarter was missing.

The teacher scolded Ramon for leaving money on top of his desk. She had the children look on the floor for the quarter. She warned them that if anyone knew what had happened to the quarter, that person should tell her before the end of the day.

Justin knew that he had made a bad choice. "What do I do now?" he asked himself.

Finish the story. Tell what Justin did.

____

____

Following God's Commands

God wants us to listen to what He asks us to do. He wants us to follow His commands and those of His Son, Jesus.

God wants us to love God with all our hearts and to love our neighbor as we love ourselves.

Jesus told us, "This is how all people will know that you are My followers, if you have love for one another."

Sometimes we do not love one another as Jesus asks us to do. We fail to love. We disobey. We lie. We take what is not ours. We do not respect what belongs to another. We blame others for our own mistakes.

When we freely choose to do these things, even though we know it is wrong to do so, we hurt members of God's family and we hurt ourselves, too. We sin.

Did You Know?
There are three kinds of sins. One kind (mortal sin) destroys our relationship with God. The other two (serious venial sin and less serious venial sin) seriously weaken or take away from our relationship with God but do not destroy it.

There are many ways to sin. Some are very serious. Others are less serious. We know that when we sin we do not love as Jesus loves.

Even though we fail, Jesus forgives our sins if we are truly sorry for them

Sin—Freely choosing to do what we know is wrong.

Jesus and Peter

Characters: Reader, Jesus, Peter; Girl, Man

Reader:
Walking along the shore one day,
Jesus called Simon Peter to come His way.

Simon, a fisherman by trade,
heard Jesus' voice and was not afraid.

He pulled up his nets,
then let them fall.
He decided to follow Jesus' call.

Across the hills, through city and town,
They preached the kingdom of God all around.

One day Jesus said,

Jesus:
"Your name is 'Rock.'
It's you I'll trust to guide My flock."

Reader:
When we love a friend,
we expect the best.
One day the Lord gave Peter a test.

Jesus:
"Do you love Me, Peter?"
said Jesus that day.
"Will you stand by Me always—come what may?"

Reader:
Peter looked at Jesus
with his eyes aglow,

Peter:
"Of course, I love You,
that You know.

I'll always be with You;
You can count on that.
Before I'd leave You,
I'd eat my hat!''

Reader:
Jesus looked sadly at
Peter, the rock.,

Jesus:
''You'll deny Me three
times before the crow of
the cock.''

Reader:
On that night before Jesus
died,
Soldiers came and took
Jesus aside.

Peter followed them to the
prison door,
Then he waited outside. He
could do no more.

He was warming himself by
the courtyard fire,
When up came a servant
girl—a girl for hire.
She said to Peter,

Girl:
''Why I know you!
You're a friend of Jesus,
isn't it true?''

Peter:
''I don't know what you are
talking about.
You're mistaken,'' said
Peter, ''without a doubt!''

Man:
''You were with Jesus,''
said another man,
''I'll bet you're a Jesus fan!''

Reader:
Then Peter cursed and screamed and pouted,

Peter:
"I don't know the man!" he finally shouted.

Reader:
At the cock's third crow,
Peter knew
What Jesus foretold had now come true.

Jesus:
"Before the cock crows,
before this night ends,
You'll say you don't know
Me—that we were never friends."

Reader:
At that moment, Jesus passed by.
He looked Peter straight in the eye.

His eyes told Peter, "I know what you've done.
But I forgive you, My friend."
Peter wanted to run.

With feelings he could no longer hide,
Peter cried and he cried and he cried and he cried.

Peter truly was sorry for failing his friend,
And he vowed to show Jesus by trying again.

Following God's Word

During the Rite of Reconciliation, before we go to the priest, we ask ourselves how well we have followed God's Word. We ask ourselves how well we have loved God and our neighbor.

We examine our conscience.

We ask ourselves about the good we have done. We ask ourselves about the good we have failed to do. We also ask ourselves about the wrong we have done. We pray about what we have done and ask God's forgiveness.

Then we tell our sins to the priest. This is called *confession.* The priest listens in Jesus' name. He helps us to think about how we have followed God's Word. He will help us learn to better follow God's Word.

Did You Know?
A priest is never free to tell what he has learned through the Sacrament of Reconciliation. He must keep secret whatever he hears. This is called the Seal of Confession.

Following Jesus' Word

Jesus says,

"If anyone wants to come with Me, he must forget himself, take up his cross everyday, and follow Me." (Luke 9:23)

"This is how all will know you for my disciples: your love for one another." (John 13:35)

Examining Your Conscience

RIGHT

Do I
Help around the house
Share my things with others
Tell the truth
Listen to my parents
Act courteously
Show respect for others
Treat others kindly
Treat others fairly
Pray
Forgive those who do me wrong

WRONG

Do I
Cheat
Argue
Put others down
Steal
Disobey
Fight
Talk back
Pout
Lie
Try to hurt those who harm me

God's Rules for Living

The Ten Commandments

1. I, the Lord, am your God. You shall not have other gods besides Me.
2. You shall not take the name of the Lord, your God, in vain.
3. Remember to keep holy the Sabbath Day.
4. Honor your father and your mother.
5. You shall not kill.
6. You shall not commit adultery.
7. You shall not steal.
8. You shall not bear false witness against your neighbor.
9. You shall not covet your neighbor's wife.
10. You shall not covet anything that belongs to your neighbor.

(*National Catechetical Directory*, Appendix A)

The Great Commandments

Love the Lord your God
with all your heart
with all your soul
with all your strength
with all your mind; and
love your neighbor as you love yourself.

(Luke 10:27; Deuteronomy 6:5; Leviticus 19:18)

Jesus' Law of Love

Love one another as I have loved you.

(John 15:12)

Let Us Pray: Keeping God's Commands

Prayer: Jesus once told about the Greatest Commandment. He said, ". . . Love the Lord your God with all your heart, with all your soul, with all your mind, and with all your strength." (Mark 12:30) When we put God first, we treat others and ourselves with love and respect. As Jesus said, ". . . Love your neighbor as yourself." (Mark 12:31) Heavenly Father, bless us with the desire to obey and come to know You. Knowing our weaknesses, we ask in faith these petitions:

Examination of Conscience and Litany

Child: *"I am the Lord, your God. Have no gods beside Me."*

Help us, Lord, to love You more than anything else in the world. For the times we put other things ahead of You,

All: forgive us, Lord.

Child: *"Do not take My name in vain."*

Help us, Lord, to always respect Your name. For the times we have sworn or used Your name in the wrong way,

All: forgive us, Lord.

Child: *"Remember to keep My special day holy."*

Help us, Lord, to worship You and keep Your day very special. For the times we failed to go to Mass on Sunday or holy days,

All: forgive us, Lord.

Child: *"Honor your father and your mother."*

Help us, Lord, to show love and obedience to our parents and to all the others who guide and care for us. For the times we failed to honor our parents and all those who care for us,

All: forgive us, Lord.

Child: *"You shall not kill."*

Help us, Lord, to live our lives fully and take care of our health and all life around us. For times we failed to do this,

All: forgive us, Lord.

Child: *"You shall not commit adultery."*

Help us, Lord, to be loving and faithful. For times of unfaithfulness,

All: forgive us, Lord.

Child: *"You shall not steal."*

Help us, Lord, to respect what belongs to others. For the times we took something that wasn't ours,

All: forgive us, Lord.

Child: *"You shall not bear false witness against your neighbor."*

Help us Lord, to speak only the truth about others. For times we lied and the times we talked bad about other people,

All: forgive us, Lord.

Child: *"You shall not covet your neighbor's wife."*

Help us, Lord, to pray often for all married couples. For the times we forget to respect married people,

All: forgive us, Lord.

Child: *"You shall not covet your neighbor's goods."*

Help us, Lord, to be satisfied with what we have and to be glad when others have good fortune. For times we were jealous or dissatisfied,

All: forgive us, Lord.

Priest: Lord, when we obey Your rules, we are loving You with our hearts, our souls, and our minds. Thank You for the gift of law and love that You gave to us. May we always follow Your guidelines. This we ask through Jesus who shows us your love. Amen.

Review Sheet 4: We Follow God's Word

Words to Know

Sin is ______________________________

Conscience is ______________________________

Examination of conscience is ______________________________

Questions to Answer

1. Are all sins harmful? ______________________________
2. Are all sins the same in seriousness? ______________________________

   ____
3. Who is hurt when we sin? ______________________________
4. Does Jesus always forgive our sin? ______________________________

   ____

Scripture to Know

"If anyone wants to come with me, he must forget ______________ . . .
and ______________ Me." (Luke 9:23–24)

Crossword Puzzle

1. Jesus called Simon ____________ to follow Him.
   (3 down)
2. Peter was a ____________________ by trade.
   (1 down)
3. Jesus gave Simon Peter the name ____________ .
   (9 across)
4. Jesus foretold that Peter would deny Him
   ______________ times.
   (7 down)
5. On the ____________ before Jesus died, _________________ took Jesus away.
   (6 across) (5 down)
6. Peter was waiting in the ____________ when a servant girl asked him if he knew ____________ .
   (8 across) (4 across)
7. When Peter heard the third crow of the ____________ , he remembered what Jesus had foretold.
   (8 down)
8. When Peter realized what he had done, he ____________ .
   (2 across)
9. Peter proved he was sorry by trying ____________ .
   (10 across)

Review

Take time to discuss these questions with your child.

- Who are some persons you want to be like? Why?
- Why do Jesus' followers want to be like Him?
- How do we show that we are followers of Jesus?
- Are we always forgiven by God?
- Peter said that he loved Jesus, but what did he do? Did Jesus still love Peter? Was Peter sorry?
- What is sin?
- When do we fail or sin?
- What can we do when we sin?
- How does the Sacrament of Reconciliation help us to say we are sorry?

Centering Prayer

Find a quiet time to lead your child in a guided meditation on Scripture.

1. Help your child to relax by taking time for slow, deep breathing.
2. Read the meditation slowly, giving the child time to recreate the Gospel scene.
3. Give sufficient time for personal prayer.

We Follow God's Word (See Matthew 26:31–35, 69–75)

Close your eyes. Take a deep breath and relax. It is night time and you are in the cold courtyard outside the building where Jesus has been taken after being arrested. In the middle of the courtyard, there is a bonfire. With Peter and some guards, you are warming your hands. Servants and soldiers move about in the courtyard. You rub your hands and then form a cup with your hands and blow warm air into them. Now you begin to feel warmer.

All at once, a large fisherman named Peter, with a curly-bearded face, looks down at you. Peter asks you to sit down on a rock beside him. You sit silently beside this strong, but sad-looking Peter.

A servant girl walks past and looks at Peter and you. She stops right in front of Peter. Pointing her finger at Peter, she says, "You were with Jesus of Nazareth!"

Peter waves her away and says, "No, not me, I was not with Jesus." Then Peter takes your hand and says, "Let's get away from her!" The girl runs over to the guards and other servants and says, again pointing at Peter, "This man is one of Jesus' followers!"

Peter lets go of your hand, turns around quickly and shouts at the girl, "No, I am not! You are so wrong!"

Peter comes back and sits down beside you on the rock. Peter stoops down, rests his head in his huge hands, and looks very frightened. Then both of you look up. Someone from the other side of the courtyard, hearing Peter speak, says again, "You must be one of them. I can tell by the way you speak that you came from the town of Galilee, too!"

Peter jumps up! He curses and screams and pouts. "I don't know the man!" he shouts. Finally, the others seem to leave him alone.

You feel very tired for it is getting late. You can hardly keep your eyes open and you yawn, but now you listen; a cock crows loud and clear—once, then twice.

Peter remembers how Jesus had said this would happen. With feelings he can no longer hide, Peter cries and cries and cries. Peter is truly sorry for failing his friend, and he vows to show Jesus that he is sorry by trying again. Jesus forgives Peter.

Now Jesus turns to you and asks you if you will promise to follow Him no matter what happens. Jesus says, "Will you follow me, N ________ ?"

I will give you a few moments to tell Jesus how you want to follow Him and be a true friend. (pause) Ask Jesus' forgiveness for times you have failed. (pause) Promise to try again. (Pause.) Hug Jesus and wave good-bye. Now open your eyes.

Action

As time allows, choose one or more of the activities given to reinforce the focus of the lesson.

Light a candle and pray together as a family. Ask God to help your family to better live Christ's love so that the world may become a better place.

At your next visit to the church, point out the baptismal font to your child. Tell your child about his or her baptismal day. Remind your child that the community is there to help us as we continue to follow Jesus.

Attend a baptism in your parish. Renew your desire to follow Jesus.

When you bless yourself from the holy water font, recall the cleansing power of water and the lifegiving power of Christ.

Resources

Children

The Hating Book by Charlotte Zolotow (New York: Harper & Row, 1969).

The Saint Book by Mary Reed Newland (New York: Seabury Press, 1979).

Swimmy by Leo Lionni (New York: Pantheon, 1963).

Adults

Christian Life Patterns by Evelyn Eaton Whitehead and James D. Whitehead (New York: Doubleday and Company, Inc., 1979).

For Parents: 5 We Show We Are Sorry
Lesson Focus: Forgiving
Goal: To help your child become more aware that God is like a loving, forgiving father.
Summary: God is a forgiving Father. The Sacrament of Reconciliation is an effective sign of His peace. In the sacrament, we express our sorrow and look for ways of showing that we are sorry for doing wrong and that we want to change our lives. The priest helps us choose an act of penance, and we accept it.
Sacramental Focus: In the Sacrament of Reconciliation, we express our sorrow and look for a way to show that we are sorry and that we want to change our lives.
Scripture Focus: "The Lord is merciful and loving, slow to become angry and full of constant love." (Psalm 103:8)
Reflection: Alienation is a feeling that most children experience, although they are seldom able to call it by name. Because they are young, because they are learning, and because they misuse freedom (just as other humans do), they often make mistakes. They fail to consider consequences. They act irresponsibly. They look for the easy way out. They act in an unkind and cruel manner. People around them are quick to let them know that their behavior is pesky, irritating, annoying, and often downright unacceptable.

Alienated children are usually not difficult to spot. Their faces are marred by furrowed frown; their eyes fail to meet yours; their voices are flat and lifeless. Their posture sags, reflecting the state of their spirit. An alienated child may be experiencing regret, anger, shame, guilt, or sorrow—and probably, to some degree, all of these. You can help your child learn to recognize, accept, and cope with these feelings. You can help your child find a way to start over again.

You can provide support in a number of ways. When you are angry with your child for something he or she has done, let your anger out. Express your displeasure, outrage, or whatever, and then let it go. Do not harbor anger and carry a lengthy grudge. Your child will not approach you for forgiveness if you make yourself unapproachable. Offer your child the opportunity to show the desire to change. Let your child know what you expect; do not make him or her guess what you would consider an appropriate way to "make up." If your child makes the first move at peacemaking, do not reject the overture: reach out and welcome your child. Let your family hear you say, "I forgive."

Through your forgiving manner, your child will come to understand that our God is merciful and forgiving, slow to anger, and full of kindness. Brought up in an atmosphere that recognizes the importance of forgiveness and reconciliation and family unity, your child will be better equipped to understand the essence of the Sacrament of Reconciliation; for the heart of the sacrament is not found in the fact that we have failed, but that God forgives.

5 We Show We Are Sorry

Joey and Jill's dad liked making tiny models out of wood. He could make trains, planes, cars, and other things with moving parts.

Once he made an entire neighborhood filled with tiny wood houses, fences, trees, sidewalks, and street lights. Now he was working on a circus.

Dad told the twins to stay away from the circus until he was finished. But one afternoon, the twins crept downstairs to the basement room where their dad worked.

First the twins just looked. Then they began to move some of the pieces around. Joey grabbed for a piece that Jill was also grabbing for.

"Give it to me," said Jill.

"I had it first," said Joey.

They began pushing and shoving each other, until the model circus tipped over and crashed to the floor.

Dad came running down the steps, but he stopped short when he saw his broken circus lying all over the floor.

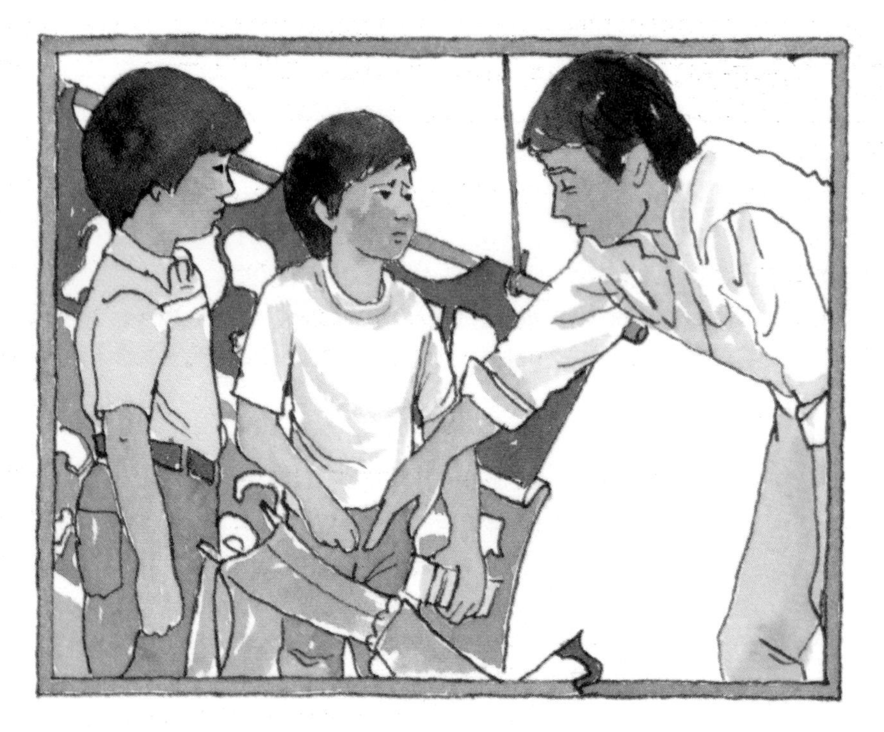

"How did this happen?" he cried.

Joey and Jill both spoke at once: "He pushed me! . . . She hit me! . . . He tipped it over! . . . It's her fault for grabbing! . . . He's a liar! . . . She's a liar!"

"Stop fighting right now," said their dad. "I am very angry with you both. I worked hard on my circus, and now it's nothing but pieces."

If you were the father, what would you do?

If you were Joey and Jill, what would you do?

What can the twins do to show that they are sorry?

Reconciliation—Sign of Peace

The followers of Jesus have a special way to say "I'm sorry." It is the Sacrament of Reconciliation.

The Sacrament of Reconciliation is a sign of peace. It is a chance to say "I'm sorry." It is a chance to start over again.

We show that we are truly sorry by telling God so. We also show God that we want to accept His loving forgiveness and change our lives by doing something good.

Jesus will help us today just as He helped people of His own time.

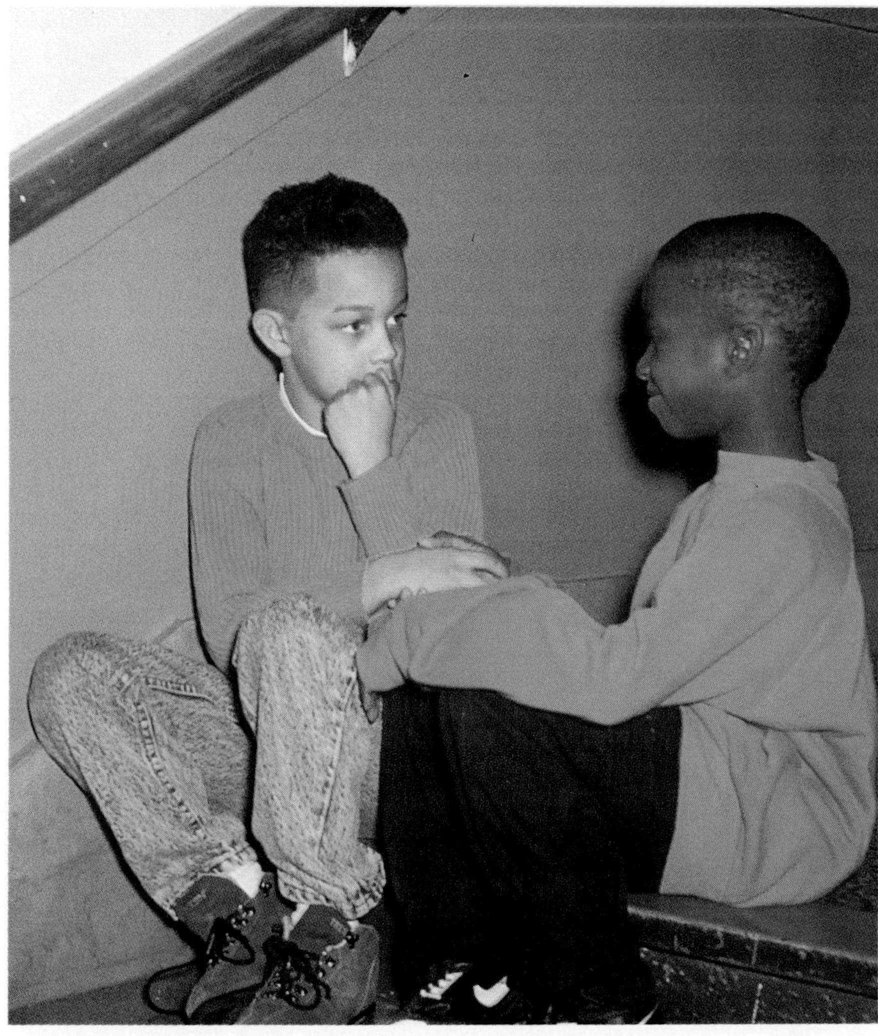

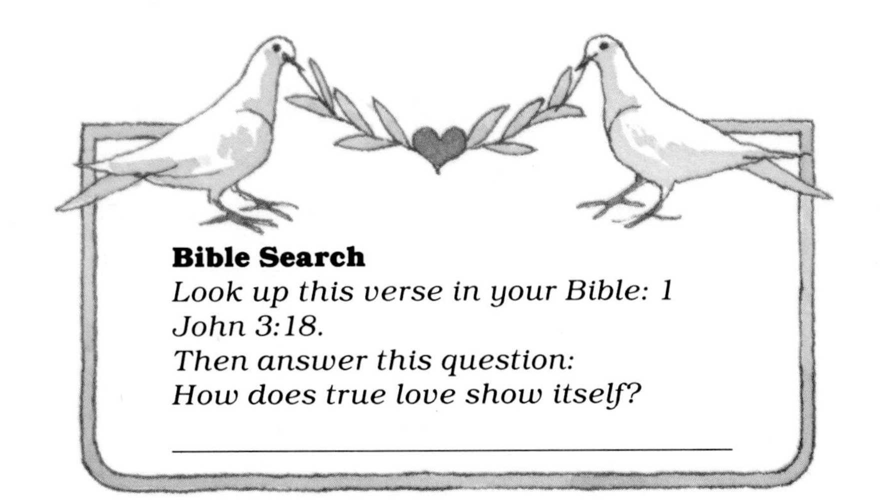

Bible Search
Look up this verse in your Bible: 1 John 3:18.
Then answer this question:
How does true love show itself?

____

Zacchaeus Finds a Way

At that time in Jericho, there lived a man named Zacchaeus. Zacchaeus was a tax collector. He made some of his money by cheating people, so people didn't like him very much.

One day Zacchaeus heard that Jesus was coming to town. He wanted to see Jesus very much. But he knew he would have a hard time.

You see, Zacchaeus was very small. Compared to him, everyone else was tall.

But Zacchaeus had a good idea. "I'll climb up that sycamore tree," said Zacchaeus. "That way, when Jesus comes down the road, I'll be able to see Him better than anyone else."

So Zacchaeus climbed up the tree and sat down among its branches, waiting for Jesus to pass by.

Jesus Calls Zacchaeus

When Jesus came by and saw the trouble that Zacchaeus had taken to see Him, He was pleased. "Zacchaeus, hurry on down from that tree. I'm going to stay in your house today!" The crowd of people didn't know what to think. "Why, Jesus is going to be a guest in a sinner's house," they said.

Zacchaeus could hardly believe that Jesus wanted to be his friend. Jesus' love made Zacchaeus feel truly sorry for his sins. He wanted to show Jesus just how sorry he was.

Zacchaeus Gives a Sign

He said to everyone listening, "Lord, I'm going to give half of all my belongings to the poor. If I have sinned by cheating anyone, I'll pay them back four times as much."

Jesus was pleased that Zacchaeus wanted to make up for the wrong he had done. He was pleased that Zacchaeus wanted to follow His way. He was pleased because Zacchaeus had found peace. (See Luke 19:1–10)

Why did Zacchaeus climb the sycamore tree?

How did Jesus show that He loved Zacchaeus?

How did Jesus' love make Zacchaeus feel?

How did Zacchaeus show that he was truly sorry for his sins?

How can we show that we are sorry for our sins?

We Show We Are Sorry

In the Sacrament of Reconciliation, we have the chance to show God that we are truly sorry for our sins. We also say that we are sorry.

We look for a way to show God that we accept His loving forgiveness and that we want to change our lives.

The priest helps us to do this. He helps us find an act of penance. It may be a prayer or a good act that shows that we really want to change.

We call the prayer of sorrow an *Act of Contrition.* We call the prayer or good act *penance.*

Penance—Something we do to show we are sorry for doing wrong.

Act of Contrition

O my God, I am sorry for my sins.

In choosing to sin and failing to do good, I have sinned against You and Your Church.

I firmly intend, with the help of Your Son, to do penance and to sin no more.

Contrition—Being sorry for doing wrong.

My Prayer of Sorrow

____

____

____

____

____

____

____

____

____

____

God Forgives

We know that God is pleased with our change of heart because of what our priest does.

He puts his hand over our head and he says, "I absolve you from your sins in the name of the Father, and of the Son, and of the Holy Spirit."

We answer: "Amen."

The Bible tells us:

"The Lord is merciful and loving, slow to become angry and full of constant love." (Psalm 103:8)

Absolve—A word meaning "take away."

Did You Know?
A sign for the Sacrament of Reconciliation is crossed keys. The keys stand for the Church's power to open and close, bind and loose. Jesus gave this power to the Church through Peter. Jesus told Peter, "I will entrust to you the keys of the kingdom of heaven. Whatever you declare bound on earth shall be bound in heaven; whatever you shall declare loosed on earth shall be loosed in heaven." (Matthew 16:19)

Amen means "Yes"—I believe. Print *Amen* on the line.

Yes, A ______________ . Yes, A ______________ . Yes, ______________ .

Prayer of Forgiveness

Can you match the saying in column A with the sentence in column B which means the same thing?

A

1. We think about what we did wrong.
2. We decide not to sin again.
3. We confess our sins to the priest.
4. We show that we are sorry for our sins.
5. Father absolves us from our sins, in the name of Jesus.

B

_____ Our priest forgives our sins in the name of Jesus.

_____ We tell the priest how we failed and why we sinned.

_____ We examine our conscience.

_____ We choose to follow Jesus and turn away from sin.

_____ We pray the Act of Contrition and we promise to do an act of penance.

Review Sheet 5: We Show We Are Sorry

Words to Know

Penance is ____ .

Absolve means "____ ."

Contrition is being __________________ .

Act of Contrition is a prayer of __________________ .

Amen means "__________________ ."

Questions to Answer

1. How can we show that we are sorry for doing wrong?

____

2. After we tell our sins to the priest, what will the priest do?

____

3. What prayer do we say right before absolution in the Sacrament of Reconciliation? ____

4. What does the priest do to show that God forgives our sins?

____

Scripture to Remember

"The Lord is merciful and __________ , slow to become __________ and full of constant __________ ." (Psalm 103:8)

"My children, our love should not be just ________ and ________ ; it must be true ________ , which shows itself in ________ ." (1 John 3:18)

Review

Take time to discuss these questions with your child.

- How do you feel when you have done something that upsets the family peace?
- What are some ways we forgive in our family?
- Can you tell me the story of Zacchaeus? How did Zacchaeus show he was truly sorry? How did Jesus show His love for Zacchaeus?
- What does the word *contrition* mean?
- Do you remember the Act of Contrition? Can you say it with me?
- What is a penance?
- What does the priest do and say to show that God forgives our sins?

Centering Prayer

Find a quiet time to lead your child in a guided meditation on Scripture.

1. Help your child to relax by taking time for slow, deep breathing.
2. Read the meditation slowly, giving the child time to recreate the Gospel scene.
3. Give sufficient time for personal prayer.

We Show We Are Sorry (See Luke 19:1–10)

Close your eyes. Take a deep breath and relax. You are entering Jericho, a small town where Zacchaeus, a tax collector, lives. The town is clean, and large sycamore trees decorate the reddish-brown dirt road. There are yellow, red, and orange flowers growing in the well-trimmed gardens. You take a deep breath of air and smell the clear, sweet-smelling aromas. You are excited to be here.

You hear the good news that Jesus, the Wonder-Worker, is coming to Jericho. You see people of all sizes and shapes gather around Jesus, Peter, James, John, and the other disciples. Mothers and fathers carrying children on their shoulders, young men and women, and children your age are running from their homes and forming a large group around Jesus. You join them but as they push forward you feel suffocated. It is hard to breathe and you are squashed in!

You then see a fat, roly-poly, well-dressed man trying to get through the crowd. You see his silk, purple and white turban and his scarf blowing in the wind. You hear him shout, "Clear the way, I want to see Jesus." People, though, do not let him through. In fact, they turn away and mumble to one other, "Zacchaeus is a cheater!" You, however, keep looking at Zacchaeus to see what he will do next. You, too, want to see Jesus. Zacchaeus runs out ahead and away from the crowd. He breaks loose. He climbs a sycamore tree. You then elbow your way out of the group and follow Zacchaeus. When you reach the sycamore tree, you stand under and lean against the tree and look up at Zacchaeus. This fat, roly-poly, short man with his silk, purple and white turban and elegant suit is sitting perched on the leafy branches of the sycamore tree. For an instant, you want to laugh, but not for too long. You are in for a big surprise.

When Jesus comes by and sees the trouble that Zacchaeus has taken to see Him, He is pleased. "Zacchaeus, hurry on down from that tree. I'm going to stay in your home today." The crowd of people don't know what to think. "Why, Jesus is going to be a guest in a sinner's house," they say.

Zacchaeus can hardly believe that Jesus wants to be his friend. Zacchaeus feels Jesus' love in his heart and he is truly sorry for his sins. He wants to show Jesus how sorry he is. Zacchaeus looks down at you and then out at everyone listening, and he shouts in a loud voice, "Lord, I'm going to give half my belongings to the poor. If I have sinned by cheating anyone, I'll pay them back four times as much."

Jesus looks right into Zacchaeus' eyes and says, "Zacchaeus I am pleased that you want to make up for the wrong you have done. I am pleased, too, that you want to follow me."

Jesus turns to you and smiles. He takes your hands, looks into your eyes, and says, "Zacchaeus believes in me and my teachings. He is willing to change his life and grow closer to me." Jesus says, "Do you believe in me? Do you want to be my friend and follow me?"

I will leave you alone with Jesus so that you can listen to Jesus and answer His question to you. Then you say good-bye to Zacchaeus, Jesus, and His friends. You thank them. You hug Jesus and say, "I am your friend. I do believe." Now open your eyes. Come back into the room.

Action

As time allows, choose one or more of the activities given to reinforce the focus of the lesson.

Sit quietly together as a family and reflect on ways to make one another happier.

Express your sorrow aloud to the family.

Accept forgiveness from others lovingly.

Take part in a parish reconciliation service.

Next Sunday at Mass, enter, in a humble reflective way, into the Penitential Rite which begins the Mass.

Resources

Children

The Alphabet Tree by Leo Lionni (New York: Pantheon Books, 1976).

Little Blue and Little Yellow by Leo Lionni (New York: Astor-Honore, Inc., 1959).

I'm Sorry by Gordon Stowell (Ventura, CA: Regal Books, 1984).

Adults

Moral Development by Ronald and Maryella Wayland (Mahwah, NJ: Paulist Press, 1975).

The Living Reminder by Henri Nouwen (New York: Seabury Press, 1977).

For Parents: 6 We Praise and Thank the Lord
Lesson Focus: Thanking
Goal: To encourage your child to thank God for the gift of forgiveness and peace that God offers in the Sacrament of Reconciliation.
Summary: God is pleased when we are truly sorry for our sins and accept God's forgiveness. God's family, the Church, is strengthened through the Sacrament of Reconciliation that brings God's peace and makes God's family one. The Church responds in thanksgiving. At the end of the Sacrament of Reconciliation, we praise and thank God and we express our willingness to start over. The priest blesses us, and we say "Amen" as a sign of thankfulness.
Sacramental Focus: At the end of the celebration of the Sacrament of Reconciliation, together with the priest, we express our thanks to the Lord for the gift of His pardon and peace.
Scripture Focus: "Give thanks to the Lord, for He is good, for His kindness endures forever!" (Psalm 106:1)
Reflection: You probably taught your child to say "thank you" long before he or she was able to appreciate its significance. Generally, very young children see themselves as the center of the world. They take for granted, moreover, as their just due, all the good things that come to them. They are not to be blamed for egocentrism, as psychology defines it. It is not a failing. They are to a great degree incapable of seeing things any other way.

Around the age of seven, however, many children begin to see things differently. They more clearly recognize centers of being outside of themselves. Their "thank you" is becoming more than a simple mechanical response. The child is becoming more capable of understanding what it means to be grateful. The child is coming to better appreciate the meaning of a gift freely given.

You can help your child to better appreciate God's gifts to His people. Take time to walk with your child and to talk about the beauties of nature that surround you. Share with your child your love for the special people in your life, and let the child know that you consider these people to be God's gifts. Together with your child, offer prayers of thanks to God for His many gifts, so that the child experiences the prayer of thankfulness even before he or she understands it.

One of God's great gifts to His Church is the Sacrament of Reconciliation. It is a sign that brings the gift of God's peace. It is a sign that God's forgiving love will make us one. It is a gift, then, that surely deserves our thanks. At the conclusion of the Sacrament of Reconciliation, we praise and thank God, and we express our willingness to start over. When the priest blesses us, we respond with an "Amen" as a sign of our thankfulness.

6 We Praise and Thank the Lord

It is good to be alive when we are at peace with our family and others. When someone we love shows us that they love and forgive us, we are happy. We want to show that we are happy. We want to say, "Thanks."

There are many ways to thank someone. Circle all the ways that you find in the word puzzle.

hug

words

letter

card

song

gift

prayer

thank

handshake

T	R	H	U	G	T	C	O	L
H	A	N	D	S	H	A	K	E
A	P	R	A	Y	E	R	I	T
N	R	U	W	O	R	D	S	T
K	A	G	I	F	T	Y	L	E
S	O	N	G	G	Y	E	E	R

How do you like to show thanks?

____

The Church Gives Thanks

When we are truly sorry for our sins, God knows we are sorry and forgives us.

All the People of God rejoice with us. Our Christian family, the Church, is better because we are forgiven.

Because we are forgiven, we want to thank God. We want to thank Him for His great gift of peace.

We want to thank Him for letting us start over, for healing us. God's love makes us stronger. God's forgiving love brings us, the members of Christ's Church, together.

Bible Search
Read Psalm 136:1–3
It tells us to give t ___________ to the Lord, because His love is

A Stranger Says "Thanks"

One day, Jesus did a favor for ten people. He healed them. He forgave them. He made them better.

Of these ten, Jesus was very pleased with one. Do you know why?

One day as Jesus was walking, He heard voices calling Him. Then He saw, standing a bit away from Him, ten people with a terrible skin disease. They were called lepers.

"Jesus, Master, take pity on us!" they cried.

Jesus looked at them with love. He said, "Go and show yourselves to the priest." As they turned away to do what Jesus said, their skin became like new again.

One of the ten, a stranger, turned back and threw himself at Jesus' feet. He cried, "Thank You, thank You, thank You!"

Jesus asked, "Where are the others? Weren't all ten of you cured? Where are the other nine? Is it only a stranger who came back to say thanks?"

Then Jesus told the man, "Go on your way. Your faith has made you whole today." (See Luke 17:11–19.)

We Are Healed

In the Sacrament of Reconciliation, Jesus offers us healing for our sins. We show that we are grateful for His gift when we praise and thank God with the priest.

Our priest says something like, "Give thanks to the Lord, for He is good."

We answer: "His mercy endures forever!"

Then the priest says to us, "The Lord has freed you from your sins. Go in peace." Or he may say, "Go in peace, and proclaim to the world, the wonderful works of God who has brought salvation."

We answer: "Amen!" Our *amen* is a sign of our thankfulness.

Amen—A word meaning "Yes, let it be!"

Reconciliation Brings Joy

God wants people to know the joy of His presence. He wants His life within us to grow and increase. We call God's life within us *grace*.

Through the Sacrament of Reconciliation, we have a sign of God's presence within us. Through the Sacrament of Reconciliation, God's grace within us grows. Through the Sacrament of Reconciliation, we come to a greater share in God's holiness and joy.

"Give thanks to the Lord, for He is good, for His kindness endures forever!" (Psalm 106:1)

Thank You, Lord!

Leader:
Give thanks to the Lord for He is good, His love is everlasting!

All:
Give thanks to the Lord!

Child:
For the beauty of the world God made,

All:
Give thanks to the Lord!

Child:
For the blessings of family and friends,

All:
Give thanks to the Lord!

Child:
For the gifts of God's love and peace,

All:
Give thanks to the Lord!

Leader:
Let us pray.

All:
Thank You, Lord, for the summer sun,
For sight and song and good deeds done.
Faith and family and loving friends,
For the day that begins,
And the night that ends.
Amen.

Review Sheet 6: We Praise and Thank the Lord

Words to know

Amen means ______________________________

Questions to Answer

1. When we are truly sorry for our sins, what are we accepting from God?

____

2. What does God's forgiving love do for the Church?

____

3. During the Sacrament of Reconciliation, how do we show that we are thankful for God's forgiveness?

____

4. When the priest says, "Give thanks to the Lord, for He is good," what do we answer?

____

Scripture to Remember

Who said: "Jesus, Master, take pity on us"? ______________________________

Who said: "Go and show yourselves to the priest"? ______________________________

Who said: "Thank you"? ______________________________

Review

Take time to discuss these questions with your child.

- How do you feel when you are forgiven?
- What do we say when we receive a gift?
- What does God do if we are truly sorry for our sins?
- How can we thank God in words? in action?
- Can you tell me the story of the ten lepers? Why did Jesus praise the one who returned to say thanks?
- What do we say after the priest absolves us from our sins?
- What does the word *Amen* mean?

Centering Prayer

Find a quiet time to lead your child in a guided meditation on Scripture.

1. Help your child to relax by taking time for slow, deep breathing.
2. Read the meditation slowly, giving the child time to recreate the Gospel scene.
3. Give sufficient time for personal prayer.

We Praise and Thank the Lord (The Grateful Leper—See Luke 17:11–19)

Close your eyes. Take a deep breath and relax. You are with Jesus and His disciples crossing the border from Galilee to Samaria. You are walking beside Matthew and right behind Jesus. You, Matthew, and the other disciples want to hurry, but Jesus stops to talk with, listen to, and bless many people along the way. Suddenly, from a distance, you hear voices calling. Who's calling? What is the group in the distance saying? Why are they so confined to one space? You and Jesus and the apostles go toward the group. Then loud and clear you hear them calling, "Jesus, Master, take pity on us!"

At their cries for help, Jesus stops. You and the other disciples stop, too, looking over the group. You even count how many are in the group: two-four-six-eight-ten. Ten in all! You look closer and see that these people have a terrible skin disease and they are very thin. You ask Matthew, "Why are these people set aside from others?" Matthew turns to you and says, "They are lepers. They have a horrible skin disease. The priest, chief of health, has a law that doesn't allow them to mingle with others. You see, their disease is very contagious. They would contaminate others. This is why they are confined to one place!" "My, they must feel sad and lonely," you think. Now Jesus walks closer to the lepers and looks at them with love. Jesus says, "Go and show yourselves to the priest." You are amazed; for you see that, as they turn away to leave Jesus, their skin becomes like new again—no scabs, wrinkles, or red swollen sores!

While Jesus, the disciples, and you follow the ten lepers who are running to the priest, you see one man break away from the group. He runs right over in front of Jesus. He throws himself at Jesus' feet. The leper, the stranger, cries, "Thank You, Thank You, Thank You!" Jesus looks at you and the other disciples and asks, "Where are the others? Weren't all ten of them cured? Where are the other nine? Is it only a stranger who comes back to say thanks?" Jesus looks down at the ground and seems disappointed. Then Jesus lifts His head, turns to the man with a loving smile and says, "Go on your way. Your faith has made you whole today."

Now you go over and stand in front of Jesus. You look into His eyes. You tell Him that sometimes you forget to say thanks for all His gifts and thanks for the many times you have sinned and have been pardoned. Jesus looks deep into your heart. He places His hands on your head in a blessing. Jesus tells you to go in peace. Take time now to ask for forgiveness and to thank Jesus for His pardon. (Pause for silent prayer.)

You go over to Jesus and whisper thanks. You hug Jesus. You tell Jesus you are sorry for all your sins. You wave good-bye. Open your eyes and come back into the room.

Action

As time allows, choose one or more of the activities given to reinforce the focus of the lesson.

Take some time this week to thank and to praise each member of your family.

Read the Bible story about the ten lepers. Look into your own heart to discover signs of gratitude.

Offer your services to the person or to the committee who plans sacramental celebrations in your parish. You might offer to help with the planning, with decorations, or with some other aspect of the celebration.

Resources

Children

Tonga and the Blue Rabbit by Ferdinand Valentine, O.P. (Chicago: Scott, Foresman & Company, 1953).

Beady Bear by Don Freeman (New York: Viking Press, 1954).

Thank You for a Drink of Water by Patricia and Victor Smeltzer (Minneapolis: Winston Press, 1983).

Adults and Children

A Family Book of Praise by Mary Jo Tully (New York: William S. Sadlier Company, 1980).

For Parents: 7 We Celebrate Reconciliation
Lesson Focus: Celebrating
Goal: To help your child review and prepare for the celebration of the Sacrament of Reconciliation, God's gift of forgiveness.
Summary: This lesson is immediate preparation for the Sacrament of Reconciliation. It is a review of all the previous lessons. It names the parts of the rite in the order in which they occur.
Liturgical Focus: The celebration of the Sacrament of Reconciliation is the Church's celebration of God's forgiving love.
Scriptural Focus: "As the Father has loved Me, so I have loved you. Live on in My love." (John 15:9)
Reflection: Children are great celebrators—much better than most adults. Because they are spontaneous creatures who tend to live life in the present, they know how to get into the spirit of celebrating. They are not bogged down by other circumstances. That Mother was angry in the morning, that their favorite game is nowhere to be found, is quickly forgotten. The present joy of celebrating outweighs all else.

It is worth remembering that celebrations serve as times to focus on the essentials of life. They are moments when divisions are to be forgotten, or healed, when those things that bind us together get the attention that they deserve. Moreover, celebrations not only focus our attention on communal peace and joy and unity, they help to create it, to develop our sense of community, to strengthen the ties that bind us.

Encourage the sense of celebration in your child. Do not pass over those family events that deserve attention and remembrance. By doing so, you will be helping your child to understand that celebration is an appropriate response to God who has blessed us with countless gifts. Among these are the gifts of His peace and forgiveness. We can experience these gifts in the Sacrament of Reconciliation.

When Reconciliation is presented within a celebration framework, children are capable of understanding the essence of this great sacrament.

Because they are quite familiar with the experience of alienation, they know the value of being forgiven. It is important that your child's first experience of the Sacrament of Reconciliation be treated by your family as a moment worthy of celebration. Do not limit the celebration to the inside of the church. Speak about reconciliation in positive terms. Make it a cause for celebration in your home. The realization that God loves us and forgives us, that He welcomes us always, that He calls us to greater growth in love is truly a reason for celebrating, and it is ultimately what the Sacrament of Reconciliation is all about.

7 We Celebrate Reconciliation

Reconciliation means "bring together again." Through the Sacrament of Reconciliation, Jesus' followers have both a sign and an experience of God's forgiveness. Here is the way Jesus' Church celebrates this sacrament.

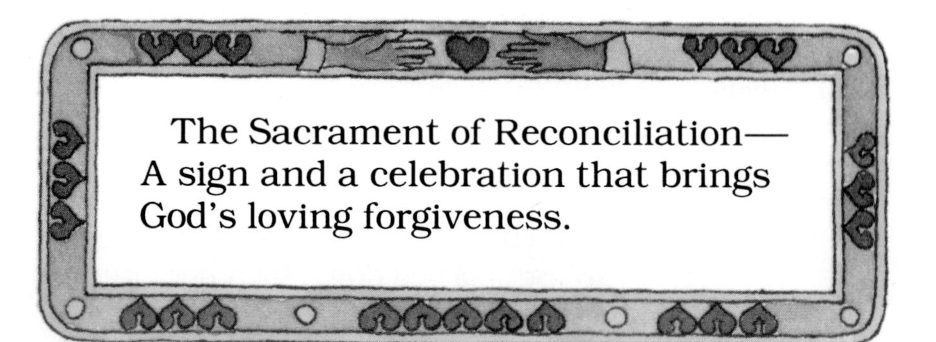

Look at the pictures on these pages. Tell what is happening in each picture.

1. I th ____________ and pr ____________ about what I have done.

2. Father w ____________________ me.

The Opening Rite

The Sign of the Cross

The Welcoming

Celebration of the Word

The Gospel Proclamation

Examination of Conscience

3. I listen to God's W ______________ .

4. I tell my s ______________ .

The Rite of Reconciliation

Confession

Absolution

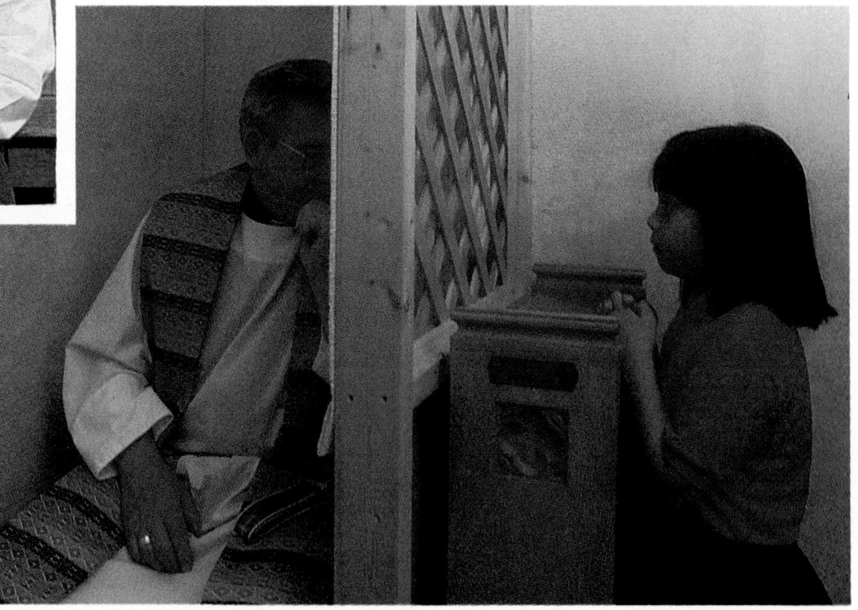

5. Father helps me find a way to show that I am sorry. I pray an Act of C ______________ .

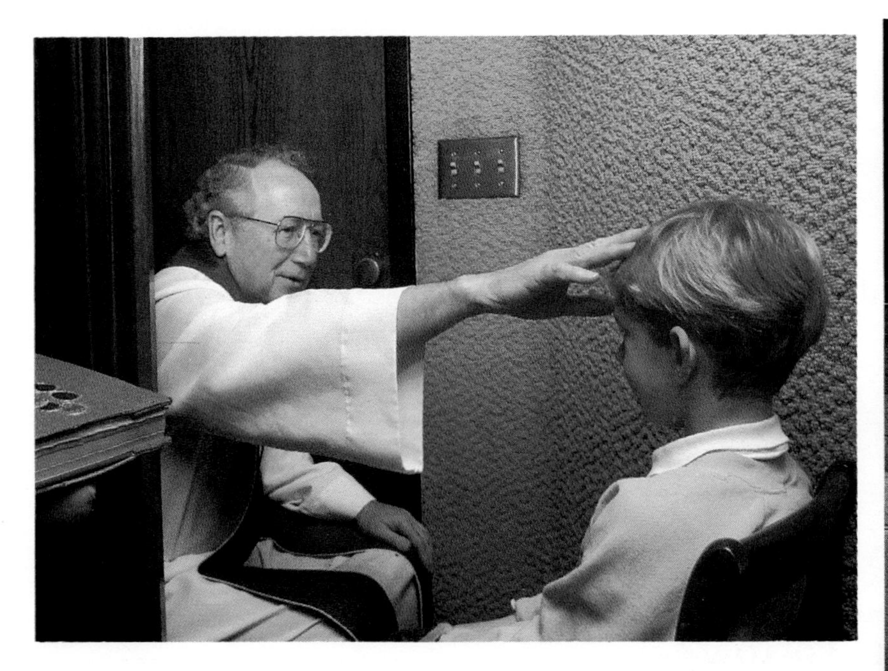

6. Father ab ____________________ me in the name of the Father, Son, and Holy Spirit.

The Closing Rite

Prayer of Thanks and Praise

Blessing and Dismissal

7. Together Father and I give th ____________ .

Jesus tells us, "As the Father has loved Me, so I have loved you. Live on in My love." (John 15:9)

Review Sheet 7: We Celebrate Reconciliation

Words to Know

Reconciliation means ____ .

Questions to Answer

1. Who welcomes me to the Sacrament of Reconciliation?

____

2. From what book may the priest read? ___________________________
3. What do I tell the priest? ___________________________________
4. Who helps me find a way to show that I am sorry and that I want to change?

____

5. What is another name for the prayer of sorrow?

____

6. What does the priest do to show that God forgives me and to bring me God's forgiveness?

____

Scripture to Remember

Jesus says:

"As the ______________ has loved _______ , so I have loved _________ .
Live on in My love." (John 15:9)

Prayer of Saint Francis

Lord, make me an instrument of Your peace,
Where there is hatred, let me sow love,
Where there is injury, pardon,
Where there is doubt, faith,
Where there is despair, hope.
Where there is darkness, light,
Where there is sadness, joy.
Lord, grant that I may not so much seek
To be consoled, as to console;
To be understood, as to understand;
To be loved, as to love.
For it is in giving that we receive;
It is in pardoning that we are pardoned;
It is in dying that we are born to eternal life.

Review

Take time to discuss these questions with your child.

- Who welcomes us when we go to confession?
- How do we begin the celebration of the Sacrament of Reconciliation?
- If the priest tells us a story about Jesus, what are we to do?
- Would you like to share your booklet on reconciliation with me? (Listen quietly to what your child has to say; do not invade the child's privacy, but listen attentively to what he or she says.)
- What prayer of sorrow will you say? Can you pray it with me now?

Centering Prayer

Find a quiet time to lead your child in a guided meditation.

1. Help your child to relax by taking time for slow, deep breathing.
2. Read the meditation slowly, giving the child time to recreate the Gospel scene.
3. Give sufficient time for personal prayer.

We Celebrate Reconciliation Reconciliation Reflection

Close your eyes. Take a deep breath and relax. You are kneeling—praying and thinking about what you have done. Jesus walks in and kneels right beside you. Jesus puts His arm around you and whispers into your ear, "I am pleased with you. I love you. My priest takes my place in the Sacrament of Reconciliation."

Now you think about what you have done: You ask, "How have I shown God I love Him? Did I pray? Did I attend Mass on Sunday and holy days? Did I listen to God's Word? How have I shown God I love others? Did I tell the truth? Did I take something that did not belong to me? Did I obey my parents and teachers? Did I fight with my brothers, sisters, or classmates? Did I make fun or talk harmfully about others?"

Now you turn and look at Jesus. You whisper to Jesus, "I am truly sorry for all my sins. I promise to try harder. Please help me, Jesus." Jesus says, "Now go and tell your sins to the priest. I will be with you. I have given My priest the power in My Name to forgive you." Now you walk over to the priest. The priest welcomes you and prays that the Father will forgive you and help you to grow. Making the sign of the cross, you pray, "Bless me, Father. . . ." Then the priest tells you a story about God's love and forgiveness. You listen to the priest. Then you tell your sins. You ask any questions you may have so that the priest can help you. The priest tells you how you can better live Jesus' Law of Love. The priest gives you a penance, an act that will help you show that you want to change your life. You pray a prayer of sorrow—Act of Contrition.

The priest places his hands over your head. He prays the words of forgiveness: "I absolve you from your sins, in the name of the Father, and of the Son, and of the Holy Spirit." You pray, "Amen." (Yes, I do believe!) With the priest, you praise God for always being ready to forgive you. The priest tells you to go in peace.

You walk back to your place. You think about the penance the priest gave you. You pray a prayer of thanks. You sit down quietly. Jesus sits beside you. Jesus puts His arm around you. You look up at Jesus. You know that you are at peace.

Now take a few moments to talk to Jesus. (Pause for silent prayer.) Wave good-bye to Jesus. Jesus is with you now as you go out to others. You join in celebrating this wonderful gift of forgiveness with your family and friends. Open your eyes and come back into the room.

Action

As time allows, choose one or more of the activities given to reinforce the focus of the lesson.

Take some time the evening before your child is to receive the Sacrament of Reconciliation to prepare in a prayerful way. Even a very short prayer, prayed in an attentive manner, can serve as a good preparation. Or you could use one of the Family Reconciliation Celebrations given in the back of this book.

If at all possible, be present as your child celebrates the Sacrament of Reconciliation. Your presence and interest will better enable your child to experience the joy of the sacrament.

Join your child in sending a thank-you note to the community, to those who helped ready the child for the sacrament, and to those who prayed for the child during the period of preparation. Do not be surprised if your note appears on the Church bulletin board.

Resources

Children and Adults

Hope for the Flowers by Trina Paulus (Mahwah, NJ: Paulist Press, 1972).

What's So Special about Today? by Andrzej Krauzc (New York: Lothrop, Lee, and Shepard, 1984).

We Forgive One Another

At an opportune time when your family is together, perhaps after the evening meal, read this passage from the Bible:

Parent:

Here is a message from St. John: "See the love God has for us . . . that we should be called children of God . . . for such we are!" (1 John 3:1)

We know the Lord Jesus' command to us: "Love one another as I have loved you." (John 13:34, adapted) Lord Jesus, we know that we belong to one another and to Your family, the Church. We know that sometimes we fail to love the members of Your family.

(Allow some time for the members of the family to think quietly about those times when they did not show love to other family members.)

Parent:

For the times we disobeyed Your law of love,

All:

Lord, forgive us.

Parent:

For the times we refused to help one another,

All:

Lord, forgive us.

Parent:

For the times we hurt one another's feelings,

All:

Lord, forgive us.

Parent:

We have sinned against You, Lord; we have also sinned against one another. We are sorry for the harm and hurt we have caused. We ask for Your help so that we may grow more like You, loving and serving one another as You loved and served us.

Sign of Peace:

Exchange a sign of forgiveness with one another, for example, a handshake, a kiss, or a hug.

Prayer:

Pray the Lord's Prayer together. You might want to hold hands as a sign of unity and mutual forgiveness.

Parent:

Lord Jesus, bless each one of us. Bless especially N ________ , who is getting ready to come to You in the Sacrament of Reconciliation. Help us all to feel Your love for us, and help us to show our love to those who surround us. Help us always to remember that the most important thing in life is to live by Your commandment, "Love one another as I have loved you."

All:

Amen.

We Say We Are Sorry

Preparation: In some comfortable yet dignified place, maybe the living room, prepare a table with a clean cloth, a candle, and a Bible prominently displayed. Place the table in such a way that it will be the focal point of the seating arrangement. When the table is ready, invite the family into the room. Once everyone is seated, light the candle.

Leader:

Please stand for our prayer. God, our Father, we the (family name) family, come before You today. You have given us many signs of Your love. We thank You for Your goodness to us.

Jesus our brother told us that He wanted us to love one another. Sometimes we fail to do that. Sometimes we are selfish and do not love others as we should. Help us to listen to what You want to tell us in the Bible. Help us to learn how to love one another better.

Reading (All sit.) Choose one: Matthew 5:23–24, Matthew 6:14–15, Luke 7:36–50, Luke 11:1–4, John 13:33–35, or John 15:9–14.

Reflection (All sit.)

Parent:

Let's think for a few minutes of a time when we were selfish or thoughtless and did something that spoiled our family's happy spirit.

(Allow some time for reflection.)

Parent:

Let us tell God and one another those things for which we are sorry.

(Each one tells what he or she is particularly sorry for. The parent begins.)

Parent:

Please stand while we say a prayer together.

God our Father, You have heard our family. Please forgive us through Jesus Christ our Lord.

All:

Amen.

Parent:

Bring us to happiness and life forever.

All:

Amen.

Parent:

Grant us Your pardon and take away our sins forever.

All:

Amen.

The Rite of Reconciliation

Examination of Conscience

We prepare for the Sacrament of Reconciliation by thinking about how we live Jesus' Law of Love. These questions can help us think about our lives.

How did I show my love for God and others?

Did I think of others? My parents?

My brothers and sisters?

My teacher and friends?

Was I kind and fair in the way I played and worked?

Did I share my things with others?

Did I care for my things? For the things of others?

Did I hurt others by telling lies or by stealing?

Did I worship God by going to Mass and taking part in the celebration?

Celebrating the Sacrament of Forgiveness

1. The priest welcomes us and prays that the Father will forgive us and help us grow.
2. The priest reads from the Word of God (optional). We think about how we have followed God's Word and Jesus' Law of Love.
3. We tell the priest our sins.
4. We listen as the priest tells us how we can better live Jesus' Law of Love. The priest gives us a penance, an act that will help us show that we want to change our lives.
5. We pray a prayer of sorrow (Act of Contrition).
6. The priest extends his hands over our head and prays the words of forgiveness, "I absolve you from your sins, in the name of the Father, and of the Son, and of the Holy Spirit." We say, "Amen."
7. We praise God for always being ready to forgive us. The priest tells us to go in peace.

Prayers to Know

Sign of the Cross

In the name of the Father, and of the Son, and of the Holy Spirit. Amen.

Trinity Prayer

Glory to the Father, and to the Son, and to the Holy Spirit.

As it was in the beginning, is now, and will be forever. Amen.

Hail Mary

Hail, Mary, full of grace,
the Lord is with you!
Blessed are you among women,
and blessed is the fruit of your womb,
Jesus.
Holy Mary, Mother of God,
pray for us sinners,
now and at the hour of our death.
Amen.

The Lord's Prayer

Our Father, who art in heaven,
hallowed be Thy name;
Thy kingdom come;
Thy will be done on earth as it is in
heaven.
Give us this day our daily bread;
and forgive us our trespasses
as we forgive those
who trespass against us;
and lead us not into temptation,
but deliver us from evil. Amen.

Act of Contrition

O my God, I am sorry for my sins.
In choosing to sin and failing to do good,
I have sinned against You and Your
Church.
I firmly intend, with the help of Your Son,
to do penance and to sin no more.

Glossary

Absolve—A word meaning "take away."

Amen—A word meaning "yes, let it be!"

Baptism—The sacrament through which we become members of God's Christian family, the Church.

Beatitudes—God's guidelines for happy living.

Bible—A special book, often called the "Word of God," through which God tells people about Himself and His love for them.

Christian—The name given to the followers of Jesus Christ.

Conscience—A God-given power within us to tell whether an act is right or wrong.

Contrition—Being sorry for doing wrong.

Penance—Something we do to show we are sorry for doing wrong.

Reconciliation—To bring together again.

Sacrament of Reconciliation—A sign and a celebration that brings God's loving forgiveness.

Sign of the Cross—Reminds us that we have been baptized in God's name and belong to God's Christian Family.

Sin—Freely choosing to do what we know is wrong.

Catechism Summary

What do Catholic Christians call the sacrament that brings God's forgiving love?
Catholics call it the Sacrament of Reconciliation.

To whom does the Sacrament of Reconciliation bring us closer?
The Sacrament of Reconciliation brings us closer to Jesus and to one another.

Who speaks in the name of Jesus and the Church when the Sacrament of Reconciliation is celebrated?
The priest speaks in the name of Jesus and the Church when the Sacrament of Reconciliation is celebrated.

Will God ever turn away from us?
God will never turn away from us when we ask forgiveness.

Through what sacrament did you become a member of God's Christian family, the Church?
Through the Sacrament of Baptism, I became a member of God's Christian family, the Church.

Do the members of God's family always act as God wants them to act?
No, sometimes they act selfishly, hurt the people who love them, and choose to do wrong.

Through what sacrament can those who belong to Jesus find peace and forgiveness?
They can find peace and forgiveness through the Sacrament of Reconciliation.

What sign reminds us that we have been baptized in God's name and belong to God's Christian family?
The Sign of the Cross reminds us that we have been baptized in God's name and belong to God's Christian family.

What are some special ways God speaks to His people?
God speaks to His people through creation, the Bible, the Church, Jesus, and through other people.

What is the Bible?
The Bible is a special book, often called the "Word of God," through which God tells people about Himself and His love for them.

When we celebrate the Sacrament of Reconciliation, when should we listen to God's Word?
We should listen to God's Word either before we talk with the priest or during the celebration of the sacrament if the priest reads from God's Word. (Whenever God's Word is read, we must listen to it carefully.)

How did Jesus say that people would know those who were His followers?
Jesus said, "This is how all people will know that you are My followers, if you have love for one another."

What is sin?
Sin is freely choosing to do what we know is wrong.

Are all sins equal?

No, some sins destroy our relationship with God (mortal sin); some sins seriously weaken our relationship with God (serious venial sin); and some sins take away from our relationship with God (less serious venial sin).

What is conscience?

Conscience is a God-given power within us to tell whether an act is right or wrong.

How do we show God that we are sorry for our sins?

We show God that we are sorry by telling God so in a prayer of sorrow and by doing something to show that we want to change our lives.

What is an Act of Contrition?

An Act of Contrition is a prayer of sorrow for sin.

What is a penance?

A penance is something we do to show we are sorry for doing wrong and want to change our lives.

What does the priest do to show that God forgives us?

The priest puts his hand over our head and says the words, "I absolve you from your sins in the name of the Father, and of the Son, and of the Holy Spirit."

Whenever we are truly sorry for our sins, what does God do?

God knows that we are sorry and God forgives us.

What word is a sign of our praise and thankfulness to God?

"Amen" is a sign of our praise and thankfulness to God.

What is the Sacrament of Reconciliation?

The Sacrament of Reconciliation is a sign and a celebration that brings God's loving forgiveness.